Dances of José Limón and Erick Hawkins

T0285366

Dances of José Limón and Erick Hawkins examines stagings of masculinity, whiteness, and Latinidad in the work of US modern dance choreographers, José Limón (1908–1972) and Erick Hawkins (1908–1994).

Focusing on the period between 1945 to 1980, this book analyzes Limón and Hawkins' work during a time when modern dance was forming new relationships to academic and governmental institutions, mainstream markets, and notions of embodiment. The pre-war expressionist tradition championed by Limón and Hawkins' mentors faced multiple challenges as ballet and Broadway complicated the tenets of modernism and emerging modern dance choreographers faced an increasingly conservative post-war culture framed by the Cold War and Red Scare. By bringing the work of Limón and Hawkins together in one volume, *Dances of José Limón and Erick Hawkins* accesses two distinct approaches to training and performance that proved highly influential in creating post-war dialogues on race, gender, and embodiment.

This book approaches Limón and Hawkins' training regimes and performing strategies as social practices symbiotically entwined with their geopolitical backgrounds. Limón's queer and Latino heritage is put into dialogue with Hawkins' straight and European heritage to examine how their embodied social histories worked co-constitutively with their training regimes and performance strategies to produce influential stagings of masculinity, whiteness, and Latinidad.

James Moreno is a choreographer and dance studies scholar who uses performance to investigate how people use their bodies to create meaning, develop communities, and respond to social systems. His choreography and research have been presented nationally and internationally. Moreno holds a PhD in Performance Studies from Northwestern University, USA, and is Associate Professor of Theatre and Dance and Dance Studies Coordinator at the University of Kansas, USA.

Routledge Advances in Theatre and Performance Studies

For more information about this series, please visit: www.
routledge.com/Routledge-Advances-in-Theatre-Performance-
Studies/book-series/RATPS

Dances of José Limón and Erick Hawkins

James Moreno

Routledge
Taylor & Francis Group

LONDON AND NEW YORK

First published 2020
by Routledge
4 Park Square, Milton Park, Abingdon, Oxon OX14 4RN

and by Routledge
605 Third Avenue, New York, NY 10017

First issued in paperback 2022

Routledge is an imprint of the Taylor & Francis Group, an informa business

Copyright © 2020 James Moreno

Publisher's Note
The publisher has gone to great lengths to ensure the quality of this
reprint but points out that some imperfections in the original copies
may be apparent.

British Library Cataloguing-in-Publication Data
A catalogue record for this book is available from the British
Library

Library of Congress Cataloging-in-Publication Data
Names: Moreno, James, author.
Title: Dances of José Limón and Erick Hawkins / James Moreno.
Description: Abingdon, Oxon ; New York : Routledge, 2020. |
Series: Routledge advances in theatre and performance studies |
Includes bibliographical references and index.
Identifiers: LCCN 2020002898 (print) | LCCN 2020002899
(ebook) | ISBN 9781138300477 (hardback) | ISBN 9780203733417
(ebook)
Subjects: LCSH: Limón, José. | Hawkins, Erick. | Choreographers–
United States–Biography. | Dancers–United States–Biography. |
Modern dance.
Classification: LCC GV1785.L515 M67 2020 (print) |
LCC GV1785.L515 (ebook) | DDC 792.80922 [B]–dc23
LC record available at https://lccn.loc.gov/2020002898
LC ebook record available at https://lccn.loc.gov/2020002899

ISBN 13: 978-1-03-247458-8 (pbk)
ISBN 13: 978-1-138-30047-7 (hbk)
ISBN 13: 978-0-203-73341-7 (ebk)

DOI: 10.4324/9780203733417

Typeset in Bembo
by Wearset Ltd, Boldon, Tyne and Wear

This book is dedicated to my beautiful wife, Cynthia. With all my love.

Contents

Figures

Introduction

Dances of José Limón and Erick Hawkins

Introduction

Dances of José Limón and Erick Hawkins examines stagings of masculinity, whiteness, and Latinidad in the work of US modern dance choreographers, José Limón (1908–1972) and Erick Hawkins (1908–1994). Focusing on the period between 1945 to 1980, this book analyzes Limón and Hawkins' work during a time when modern dance was forming new and controversial relationships to academic and governmental institutions, mainstream markets, and notions of embodiment. The prewar expressionist tradition championed by Limón and Hawkins' mentors faced multiple challenges as ballet and Broadway complicated the tenets of modernism and emerging modern dance choreographers faced an increasingly conservative postwar culture framed by the Cold War and Red Scare. By bringing the work of Limón and Hawkins together in one volume, *Dances of José Limón and Erick Hawkins* accesses two distinct approaches to training and performance that proved highly influential in establishing postwar relationships between choreographers and institutions, market forces, and notions of embodiment.

Before forming their own dance companies, Limón and Hawkins danced with two of the most influential modern dance choreographers of the twentieth-century: Limón with Doris Humphrey and Hawkins with Martha Graham. After forming his own company, Limón embraced and adapted Humphrey's prewar expressionist strategies, which aligned his work with burgeoning dance institutions and market forces. He also maintained an intimate working relationship with Humphrey, making her Artistic Director of his company, a post she held until her passing. Conversely, Hawkins' abandonment of prewar expressionistic strategies, coupled with his integration of kinesiological approaches to training and notions of embodiment put him at odds with dance institutions and market forces. Additionally, his explosive romantic break-up with Graham resulted in his excommunication from Graham's powerful circles of influence. Although this book touches on Limón and Hawkins' prewar beginnings, the focus is on their distinct paths from the founding of their respective companies and their influence on postwar dance.

José Limón

José Arcadio Limón was born in 1908 in Culiacan, Mexico. His father, a musical conductor, was of Spanish and French descent and his mother was Mexican with a Yaqui Indian ancestry. The Limón family fled the Mexican Revolution in 1915, eventually settling in Los Angeles, California. Limón studied visual art at UCLA for one year before moving to New York City in 1928 to pursue a career as a painter, a career that did not come to fruition. Through the guidance of high school friends, Limón began taking classes at the studio of Doris Humphrey and Charles Weidman. Within his first year of study, Limón and Weidman began a romantic relationship, which lasted until 1940. Their breakup was the primary reason for Limón's departure from the Humphrey/Weidman dance company in 1940.

After leaving Humphrey/Weidman, Limón moved to California's San Francisco Bay area and began working with former Martha Graham Company member, May O'Donnell. In 1941 Limón married Pauline Lawrence, former costumer, business manager, and accompanist for the Humphrey/Weidman Dance Company. Limón and Lawrence moved back to New York in 1942 and Limón began to once more work with Humphrey. In 1943 Limón was inducted into the United States Army, where he choreographed several works for the Special Services until his release in 1945. He received a Certificate of Naturalization on January 20, 1947. Limón founded the José Limón Dance Company in 1946, with Doris Humphrey as Artistic Director; Lucas Hoving, and Betty Jones, as company members; and Pauline Koner as guest artist. In 1969 Limón gave his final stage appearance, performing "The Leader" in *The Traitor* and "The Moor" in *The Moor's Pavane*. He died from cancer three years later.

Erick Hawkins

Born in Trinidad, Colorado, in 1909, Hawkins' dance career began with a brief summer apprenticeship under Harald Kreutzberg in 1933. Upon returning to the US Hawkins studied at George Balanchine's School of American Ballet from 1934–1938. From 1936–1938 he performed and choreographed as a member of Lincoln Kirstein's Ballet Caravan. He joined the Martha Graham Dance Company in 1938, becoming the first male dancer to do so. He began a 12-year romantic partnership with Graham, marrying in 1948 and divorcing in 1954. Hawkins founded the Erick Hawkins Dance Company in 1951, the same year he met the musical composer, Lucia Dlugoszewski whom he married in 1962. Dlugoszewski became Hawkins' primary collaborator, working together throughout their careers.[1] In the mid-1950s, Hawkins discovered Mabel Todd's book, *The Thinking Body* which prompted his exploration into a new methodology of training and performing based on the nascent field of ideokinesis. (Ideokinesis engages relationships between the neuro-musculo-skeletal system and one's mental states.) Hawkins' innovative training techniques, performance techniques, and choreographic methods proved highly influential in shaping dance discourse from the mid-twentieth century onward.

Limón in literature

Limón entered modern dance literature in the 1930s through reviews of his performances as a company member with the Humphrey/Weidman Dance Company. Beginning in the mid-1940s and continuing throughout his career, Limón also wrote himself into modern dance literature by contributing articles and essays into dance periodicals, chapters into books, and an unfinished memoir. His early writings typically discuss compositional methods and performance techniques, while his later writings of the 1950s and 1960s begin to historize the genre; discuss how modern dance might establish itself as an American artform; and the state of dance within culture and society. Limón began writing his memoirs in the late 1960s on his farm near Stockton, New Jersey as he cared for his wife, Pauline Lawrence Limón during her final bout with cancer. Limón continued writing after her death, but when he died in 1972, his memoirs remained unfinished. They were inherited by Charles Tomlinson, costumer and close friend of Limón, who donated them to the Dance Collection at the New York Public Library. They were edited by Lynn Garafola under the title *José Limón: An Unfinished Memoir* (1998).

In the late 1940s, Limón started appearing in "dance history" texts such as Margaret Lloyd's *The Borzoi Book of Modern Dance* (1949), Jill Johnston's *The New American Modern Dance* (1965), Don McDonagh's *The Rise and Fall and Rise of Modern Dance* (1970), and Selma Jean Cohen's *Doris Humphrey: An Artist First, An Autobiography* (1972). In these early texts, Limón was regularly positioned as a leader of postwar choreographers who perpetuated expressionist values of pre-war choreographers. He was also regularly portrayed as a powerful performer whose Latino heritage brought a "proud and noble" bearing to the male dancer. These portrayals dominated writings on Limón until the mid-1990s when an examination of gender and sexuality in Limón's *The Moor's Pavane* (1949) appeared in Ramsay Burt's *The Male Dancer: Bodies, Spectacle, and Sexuality* (1995). In the mid-2000s a more thorough examination of Limón begins with Susan Manning's *Modern Dance, Negro Dance: Race in Motion* (2004). Manning examines Limón's particularly complicated position within modern dance's black/white binary as well as his position as a queer man within heteronormative viewing conventions. In *A Game For Dancers: Performing Modernism in the Postwar Years* (2006) Gay Morris examines Limón's place within the genre of modern dance as the narrative forms of prewar dance, brought to its apex by Limón and Graham, were challenged by a new "objectivism" exemplified by the works of Merce Cunningham, John Cage, and Alwin Nikolais. In *The People Have Never Stopped Dancing: Native American Modern Dance Histories* (2007), Jacqueline Shea Murphy examines Limón and his work in relation to his Mexican and Native-American heritage and how this relationship allowed Limón to become a role model for Native-American choreographers and dancers. And finally in *How to do Things with Dance: Performing Change in Postwar America* (2010), Rebekah Kowal explores how Limón's performances can be read as dissident stagings of heteronormative family life and queerness.

Hawkins in literature

Like Limón, Hawkins entered modern dance literature through reviews of his performances. Reviewers covering the Martha Graham Dance Company regularly commented on Hawkins as a powerful masculine presence that broadened the scope of Graham's company and work. And similar to Limón, Hawkins started appearing in "dance history" texts such as Margaret Lloyd's *The Borzoi Book of Modern Dance* (1949) and Don McDonagh's *The Rise and Fall and Rise of Modern Dance* (1970). Hawkins began to write himself into the modern dance archives in the mid-1940s and continued throughout his career, contributing articles and essays into dance periodicals that culminated in his 1992 book, *The Body Is a Clear Place* in which he articulates his kinesiologically based approach to training and choreography.

Unlike Limón, there is a dearth of critical analysis on Hawkins' work. The overwhelming majority of texts are apologias to Hawkins' choreography, praising him and decrying the ways he was overlooked. *Five Essays on the Dance of Erick Hawkins*, edited by Gordon Norton in 1980, is exemplary of this ouevre. Five champions of Hawkins make the case for the importance of his work within the context of his more renowned postwar colleagues. Another set of writings focus on Hawkins' revolutionary infusion of kinesiological approaches into modern dance. These texts go into detail on the anatomical approaches Hawkins introduced to modern dance, but do not discuss how they circulated within culture and society. This category culminates in Renata Celichowska's, *The Erick Hawkins Modern Dance Technique* (2000) in which Celichowska discusses particulars of the Hawkins' Technique with tangential discussions on Hawkins' philosophical foundations.

The solitary critical study on Hawkins is Mark Franko's, *Martha Graham in Love and War* (2012) in which Franko explores Hawkins' work while with Graham and her company. Franko does much to reveal the unrecognized contributions that Hawkins made to Graham's work as a choreographer, colleague, and administrator. For example, Franko writes how Hawkins secured composers and the rights to their music, booked tours, and choreographed many of his own roles in some of Graham's most well-known dances. Franko also discusses Hawkins' independent choreography while with Graham.

Gender and sexuality

In discussing Limón, Hawkins, and their dances, I emphasize the term "queer." Unlike "gay" or the more pathologized "homosexual," "queer" avoids positioning these choreographers and their

work in direct opposition to a monolithic "heterosexuality." It also
elides the notion of an essentialized "homosexuality" formed
through, or as a product of heteronormativity.[2] Rather than this
entrenched oppositional duality of homosexual/heterosexual, I argue
that Limón and Hawkins worked within, moved through, and
represented multiple sites. Their performances of masculinity and
non-normative sexuality both reified and resisted the marginalized
subcultures and privileged centers with which they were associated.
"Queer" is more adaptable than "homosexual" or "heterosexual" to
argue for this complicitous and resistant relationship to regulatory
codes and conventions. I realize that my use of "queer" as unstable,
open, and non-normative is open to the critique that I do not ade-
quately scrutinize power relationships between "homosexuality" and
"heterosexuality," or that I usurp "queerness" as a position from
which to represent "gay" men.[3] I am not attempting to speak for a
"gay," "homosexual," or "bisexual" culture. Rather, I use "queer"
with the hope to engage in social and political strategies shared by
people working in dissident ways.[4]

"America," culturally marked, and universal

I understand the term "America" to be an imperialist, ideological
construction, in which the United States uses the name to describe
itself while simultaneously claiming the entire Western hemisphere. I
use the term American anachronistically, to align it with the way
that Limón and Hawkins used it to describe themselves and the
artform of American modern dance. Furthermore, I refer to Limón
as Mexican or Mexican-American, but not as Latino or Latinx,
partly because he did not use that term himself and partly because it
was not in wide circulation during his life. Neither do I refer to
Limón as Chicano, again because he did not identify as such and also
because he was not directly involved in Chicano activities.[5] Person-
ally, I identify as Mexican-American and Latino, to align my work
with ideas that resist United States imperialist practices and to build
connections with this dissident Latino heritage, both past and
present.

I refer to Hawkins as European-American, white, or *culturally
unmarked*, after dance historian, Susan Manning.[6] I use the term
culturally marked body to refer to a body that is marked as different
from dominant and normative cultures. For example, in the postwar
period explored in my project, the male European-American, or

white male body, was the embodiment of the dominant normative culture in the United States. This positioned a white male, such as Hawkins, as a culturally unmarked body and Limón, a culturally marked body.

Methodology

My research methods emerge from my approach to dance studies as an interdisciplinary field within the humanities and social sciences. My choreographic analysis is an intertextual examination of evidence and sources such as live performances, videos and films of dances, choreographic notes, dance reviews, interviews, notated choreographic scores, written texts, music, etc. I also incorporate cross-genre approaches in which I analyze Limón and Hawkins' work in the context of and in relation to social and theatrical dance and Western and non-Western dance.

Additionally, I examine relationships between dance and theatre, literature, visual art, and studies of movement culture. I use stage histories and performance reconstructions of Limón and Hawkins' dances to analyze relationships between reconstructions of dance and ideas of originality and authenticity as well as how Limón and Hawkins' dances circulated in the dance world. Through these methods, I analyze Limón and Hawkins' use of choreographic structure and style, relationship of movement to music, audience reception and spectatorship, spatial relationship of dancers to each other and to the stage space.

I augment these approaches with ethnographic and autoethnographic methods that draw on my experiences and training as a dance practitioner. These include taking classes and workshops in both Limón and Hawkins Techniques, as well as in multiple kinesiological-based approaches to dance and movement. Additionally, I have performed Limón's choreography as well as his mentor, Doris Humphrey.[7] I integrate these practice-based experiences with personal interviews of current and former Limón and Hawkins Dance Company members and associates. Writing at this confluence of practice and scholarship, I regard my training and experiences as epistemological practices that are not exclusive, but rather inclusive and fluid, each experience regularly informing and affecting others.

Periodization

My project recognizes Limón, Hawkins, and their postwar colleagues as modern dance choreographers who were different in degree, not kind. For example, I approach both Humphrey and Cunningham as modern dance choreographers rather than Humphrey as a modern expressionist and Cunningham as post-modernist. In doing so, I follow Susan Manning's periodization of American modern dance in which 1930 to 1980 is designated as "modern dance," using the predominant terminology spearheaded by John Martin in 1930 as the genre's beginning, to its ending in the contemporary practices of the 1980s.[8] And like Manning, as well as Rebekah Kowal, I examine the early 1940s as a pivotal point of change for the art form, as opposed to the standardized narrative that locates 1930 and 1960 as major junctures in the genre.

I do not recognize postmodernity in American modern dance until the early1980s, when choreographers focused on ways bodies represented the social world rather than how postmodernity was developed through medium-specificity and formalism. The choreography of Bill T. Jones provides an example. Unlike the avant-garde choreographers of the 1960s and 70s, Jones's performances and choreography do not descend from an assumed universal "white" body, but ascend from the attributes of the particular body performing. The particular, rather than the universal, becomes the fundamental element in dance composition.

Principles of selection

Some of the dances I discuss were available online or on DVD which allowed for an analysis built on repeated viewings. Other dances, as well as lecture demonstrations, workshops, and classes were viewed in library archives. I have also viewed several works live. My hope is that my analysis of these dances will benefit dance studies not only as a source for future researchers, but also as a teaching tool.

Chapter summaries

Chapter 1: recovering Hawkins

The focus of this chapter is to recover and reimagine Hawkins' work and his impact on the field of modern dance. The author begins by examining Hawkins' development as a choreographer during his 12-year tenure with The Martha Graham Dance Company, as well as the repercussions of his break with her as both lover and colleague. Hawkins' abandonment of Graham's choreographic approaches and incorporation of kinesiology into his technique and theory of embodiment are analyzed for the ways they intervened in expressionistic conventions and pioneered somatic approaches to training. Hawkins' collaborative processes and partners are explored with a focus on the musical composer, Lucia Dlugoszewski who Hawkins met in 1951 and married in 1962. Finally, the author explores Hawkins' position within postwar modern dance as he moved between the expressionist schools led by Graham and Limón and the avant-garde schools of Merce Cunningham, John Cage, and the Judson Church choreographers.

Chapter 2: Limón's biblical dances

The second chapter examines how Limón's biblical story ballets cut across categories of gender and sexuality to re-shape notions of heteronormativity. As a prominent figure in the shift from prewar to postwar dance, Limón's stagings of gender and sexuality revealed many of the tensions and contradictions choreographers encountered in an increasingly conservative culture framed by the US Cold War and Red Scare. Focusing on his dance, *The Traitor* (1954), this chapter examines Limón's staging of biblical narratives as frameworks to perform a non-normative masculinity. The author shows how Limón used biblical story ballets to complicate postwar notions of gender by heightening the visibility of male dancers; intensifying heteronormative anxieties; broadening opportunities for more nuanced and ambiguously gendered male characters; and staging more complex and intimate same-sex partnerings and groupings.

Chapter 3: Plains Daybreak

Chapter 3 works in tandem with Chapter 4 to examine stagings of race and notions of minstrelsy in Limón and Hawkins' dances. After World War II the practice of drawing on "Oriental" and non-Western cultures as source material for choreography was drawing to an end and self-representations by non-white choreographers was steadily growing. As bridges between pre- and postwar practices, Limón and Hawkins' dances, in which they represent cultures other than their own, work at the cusp of these changes. Focusing on Hawkins' 1979 dance *Plains Daybreak*, this chapter examines Hawkins' incorporation of Native-American cultures into his work. The author explores Hawkins' "right" to artistic freedom as notions of cultural relativism was gaining ground.

Chapter 4: Brown in black and white: José Limón dances The Emperor Jones

As mentioned above, this chapter works in tandem with Chapter 3 to examine stagings of race and minstrel-based practices. This chapter examines Limón's 1956 dance, *The Emperor Jones*, based on Eugene O'Neill's 1920 play of the same name. The author examines the transition of minstrel-based practices from prewar to postwar modern dance, with a focus on Limón's choice to put himself and his all-male cast in black body paint. The author examines how Limón's Mexican ancestry and white modernist dance heritage converged to reveal American identity as a composition of shifting presences and absences that continually intersected and diverged. Limón's painted body is explored as a tripled body; a brown Mexican body; a white "American" body (with the privilege to represent the Other); and the black body of Brutus Jones.

Notes

1 When asked about the start date of The Erick Hawkins Dance Company, Hawkins replied,

> you can't say the company was founded because it just grew ... In '51 I started the school ... when I had it totally on my own ... Well I think it's better to take it from the time of the first performance, '52.
> (Hawkins, Erick. Interview by Sears, May 27, 1983)

The Erick Hawkins Dance Company website dates the founding of the company as 1951.
2 Warner, Michael, and Social Text Collective. *Fear of a Queer Planet: Queer Politics and Social Theory*. Minneapolis, MN: University of Minnesota, 1993.
3 Manning, Susan. "Looking from a Different Place: Gay Spectatorship of American Modern Dance." In *Dancing Desires: Choreographing Sexualities On and Off the Stage*, edited by Jane Desmond. Durham, NC: Duke University Press, 2001.
4 I have used quotation marks around terms referring to gender and sexuality in this section to emphasize their constructed-ness. However, I discontinue using quotation marks after this section.

5 I align my work with Rafael Perez-Torres' description of Chicano. He writes,

> the term was first employed in the 1960s and 1970s as a name of self-affirmation and empowerment, its current use is much more problematic. In California and Arizona, the term has a political and social charge that is does not have in places like New Mexico or even Texas, where individual may reject the term "Chicano" in favor of "Hispano" or "Mexicano" or "Texano." There are generational differences as well ... The terminology, in short, is vexed and I acknowledge the conundrum of identification and naming that is Chicano or Chicana.
> (Perez-Torres, *Mestizaje: Critical Uses of Race in Chicano Culture* 221)

6 Manning, Susan. *Modern Dance, Negro Dance: Race in Motion*. Minneapolis, MN: University of Minnesota Press, 2004.

7 Humphrey acted as Artistic Director of the José Limón Dance Company from its inception in 1946 to her death in 1958.

8 Manning, Susan. *Modern Dance, Negro Dance: Race in Motion*. Minneapolis, MN: University of Minnesota Press, 2004.

Chapter 1

Recovering Hawkins

Introduction

Dance scholar Naomi Prevots writes, "when history records great American artists of the twentieth century, Hawkins will be at the top of the list."[1] Although modern dance historians have been working assiduously since Prevots' proclamation, Hawkins has yet to gain the notoriety she predicted. From the university courses I teach, to the broader field, many students and practitioners are unfamiliar with Hawkins and his impact on the field. This chapter joins those endeavoring to recover Hawkins' work. While this chapter occasionally touches on Hawkins' prewar work, the focus is on his postwar career, particularly the development of his dance technique.

Hawkins began his dance career in ballet, but the major influence on his postwar work was his relationship with Graham as both her romantic and professional partner. This chapter explores how his relationship with Graham was influenced by a complicated connection with Graham's mentor, lover, and colleague, Louis Horst. When Hawkins joined the Graham Company in 1938, Graham was in the process of choreographing *American Document*, a dance that would signal a new direction for her, one built on a narrative-based theatricality rather than Horst's demand for abstraction. Although Graham and Horst had been drifting apart both romantically and professionally, their final romantic break coincided with Hawkins' induction into the company.

Louis Horst

Horst never wrote music for Hawkins or Limón and neither Hawkins or Limón took the almost obligatory step of taking Horst's composition classes.[2] However, through his broad influence in prewar dance Horst nevertheless played a role in both Hawkins' and Limón's development. Horst's own career underwent a major shift when he left Denishawn in 1925. When asked why he left, Horst replied, "several reasons. One, they [Denishawn] were going to the Orient for a year and a half. And I had eleven years of playing mostly Oriental music. Picking things off of Oriental records. And I also felt that there's something new going on ... So, I decided to go to Vienna instead to study composition."[3] Horst planned to stay in Vienna for two years and study with Ricard Stöhr, a theorist recommended to Horst due to Stöhr's interest in dance. However, he did not find the vital and innovative spirit he hoped for and cut his stay to five months. He commented that American artists were "waking up and that people didn't always have to go to Europe just to learn music. That was a hang up from my childhood. And I got Europe out of my system, once and for all."[4]

Horst's time in Vienna could be characterized as part of his ongoing mission to discover new directions in art. Horst had always been, from his early days with Denishawn, a key figure in gathering and distributing news and information about European avant-garde musicians, painters, and dancers. Since German modern dance was of particular interest to American modern dancers, Horst would translate articles in German newspapers, with an attentive eye on Mary Wigman's ideas of dance as an independent art. Wigman's notion that art emerged from one's own experience or emotions, rather than an outside source such as music or theatre, was vibrating with a revolutionary immediacy.

Like Horst, Graham did not go on Denishawn's 1925 "Oriental tour" and when Horst returned from Vienna, they immediately began working together. Horst urged her to produce a concert of her work, which she did in 1926. While Horst and Graham's subsequent professional and romantic partnership is well known, less so is his prominence in the 1930s dance scene in a more general way. In addition to his work with Graham, Horst was also key in Humphrey's emergence as an independent choreographer. Horst saw Humphrey regularly while she was teaching at Denishawn's New York school in 1928. As he did with Graham, Horst admonished Humphrey to work independently. He recalls:

I said listen, you've *got* to break away from Denishawn! You've *got* to do your concerts and she always said, no, no, Martha is wrong, Denishawn is right ... But one time I took Pauline

[Lawrence] and Doris to dinner and I talked for about two hours. And the next couple of days Pauline said, well Doris has decided she is going to give a concert. She said you won her over the other night. So, Doris gave her first concert early part of the autumn in 1928.[5]

With Humphrey breaking the Denishawnian bonds, Horst's two most significant mentees were on their way. In addition to Graham and Humphrey, Horst also played, advised, mentored, and conducted for most of the prominent New York choreographers of the 1930s. This included: Charles Weidman, Helen Tamiris, Agnes de Mille, Harald Kreutzberg, Michio Ito, Ruth Page, and Adolph Bolm. As Horst recalls, "I played for them all. I used to rehearse in five different studios in a day. I'd start off in the morning and rehearse with Doris, then go to Tamiris, go to Martha, go back to Charles" (Horst Interview, 1958). Horst first played for Kreutzberg in 1928, when Kreutzberg and Tilly Losch came to New York in Max Reinhardt's production of *The Miracle*. Horst recalled, "We rehearsed in Martha's studio. That's how Martha and I got so friendly with them, and I played their first concert."[6] And when Kreutzberg returned in 1929, this time with Yvonne Georgi, Horst again accompanied.

Kreutzberg played a pivotal role in both Hawkins and Limón's lives, as both cite their viewing of him as the most powerful experience propelling them into dance. Hawkins was still a student at Harvard when he saw Kreutzberg for the first time. He writes:

> I saw a big three-sheet [poster] in front of the theater, it's torn down now, of two dancers, Harald Kreutzberg and Yvonne Gyroki. I literally did not know that there was such a thing as dancing on the stage. I had gone to see plays and heard music in Kansas City, but I did not know there was anything such as you'd call the art of the dance. It's that new. I came back that night. I remember sitting in the front row, because I had little money at that time. And when I came out at the first intermission, I remember talking to myself. I said, that's what I'm going to do.[7]

And Limón writes that seeing Kreutzberg,

> simply and irrevocably changed my life. I saw the dance as a vision of ineffable power. A man could, with dignity and a

towering majesty, dance. Not mince, prance, cavort, do "fancy dancing" or "show-off" steps. No: dance as Michelangelo's visions dance and as the music of Bach dances.[8]

Other than Shawn, there were few examples of "proto-modern" male dancers that could provide inspiration for up-and-coming dancers. Captivated by Kreutzberg's performance of a powerful and profound masculinity, both Hawkins and Limón began to see how dance could be a legitimate profession for men.

After graduating from Harvard, Hawkins searched for a dance instructor and in the summer of 1933, with financial support from a patron, traveled to Salzburg, Austria to study with Kreutzberg. He was there for a little over a month before returning to the States. While Hawkins recalls his time with Kreutzberg fondly, it does not seem to have been a deeply formative experience. Hawkins comments:

> Toward the end of the summer I took him to tea one day and I said Mr. Kreutzberg do you think I can be a dancer? He said, Well I think so. He said you can't study with me because I'm a small man and you're a big man. I'm touring, I'm not going to be teaching all the time. So I remember saying, so what should I do? And this is, I never understood what he meant. He said study ballet for six months and then forget it. And I don't know what he meant.[9]

Although Kreutzberg's advice felt cryptic to Hawkins, he did end up, in a way, following it by beginning studies in Balanchine's School of American Ballet and then Lincoln Kirstein's Ballet Caravan. From their formative Kreutzbergian moments to the end of their careers, both Hawkins and Limón remained invested in developing a credible and mature identity for male modern dancers.

Beginning again

From his choreographic beginnings with Ballet Caravan; to the dances he made while with Graham; and on to his founding of The Erick Hawkins Dance Company; Hawkins' search for his unique choreographic voice was a long one. During his tenure with the Graham Company, from 1938–1950, Hawkins choreographed fourteen dances: ten solos, two duets, and a trio. There are no surviving films or notation for any of these dances. Only *Trickster Coyote* (1941) and *John Brown* (1947) were revised by Hawkins for his own company.[10] The first dance Hawkins choreographed under the auspices of The Erick Hawkins Dance Company was a solo for himself, *openings of the (eye)* (1952). After *openings of the (eye)*, Hawkins presented three more dances in 1952, all solos for himself. These four dances were followed by a five-year gap before his seminal duet, *Here and Now with Watchers* (1957). There was then a three-year break before his equally significant duet, *8 Clear Places* (1960). It is in these two pieces, *Here and Now with Watchers* and *8 Clear Places*, that his unique artistic vision coalesces and forms a foundation for his subsequent work. In 1961 Hawkins choreographed the quartet, *Early Floating* which marks the beginning of his signature released and flowing style. It also marks the beginning of his consistent production of group dances that continued throughout his career.

While the 1950s acted as a kind of gestation period or decade of new directions for Hawkins, it was, arguably, Limón's most fertile and productive period. When Graham disbanded her company in 1950 and 1951, she left a vacuum in the genre. With the resounding success of *The Moor's Pavane* in 1949, Limón and his company advanced into the limelight and became the leading company of the day, a position he would share with Graham throughout the 1950s. Limón was widely recognized as the postwar heir to Graham and Humphrey's expressionist tradition. He became the choreographer most responsible for augmenting and adapting their work for a growing modern dance audience. For example, Jill Johnston writes that Limón's choreography was "a culmination of the early era … in which the percussive accents of his predecessors were smoothed out in fluid articulations."[11] While Johnston was writing about Limón specifically, it's important to remember that Limón was not working alone. After leaving the Humphrey/Weidman Company in 1940 Limón moved to California, but returned to New York in 1942 and developed a new working relationship with Humphrey. In 1946, when Limón formed the José Limón Dance Company, he named Humphrey Artistic Director. It was a post she held until her death in 1958, guiding Limón through his most significant, productive, and innovative period. And while Limón's reliance on Humphrey's advice and feedback faded in the last year of their partnership, his most widely circulating works cannot be considered without acknowledging her influence.

Conversely, when Hawkins and Graham separated in 1950, they never again worked together. Their relationship as both lovers and colleagues made for a highly dramatic break, which left Hawkins on the wrong side of many of his closest associates and friends. This was not a particularly novel position for Hawkins. From the time he joined the Graham Company in 1938, he was involved in multiple ongoing antagonistic relationships. Many of Graham's all-female group saw Hawkins' induction into the company as a disruption of their powerful sisterhood, some viewing him as an interloper who replaced them in Graham's affections. To make matters worse, under Graham's direction, Hawkins rehearsed the dancers within his first month in the Company, which sparked resentment among the dancers who had already danced with Graham for years. And finally, Hawkins' introduction of ballet into the company was unwelcome. Some felt the integration of ballet promoted a loss of feminist power both individually and as a community. Former Graham dancer Jean Erdman summarizes:

> I mean now-a-days there's women's lib and everything, but there was women's lib right there! You know, right there! We were the whole thing, the whole thing [feminine and masculine]. So, when this man [Hawkins] walks in and Miss Graham starts to do these mincing little steps and she starts to do *drama* and we have to put on shoes and we have to come down lightly on the floor instead of *Ooom*, you know. Everybody's pulling faces, what's going on with Martha? And of course, Louis Horst didn't care for it either. Because he used to be the only man. And the technique started to change.[12]

Hawkins' tumultuous time with Graham and her company concluded with his volatile departure that left him blackballed by the powerful circle of Graham dancers, collaborators, and supporters. As he comments, "when I broke away in '50 and started out ... I had no friends. You see I was absolutely friendless."[13] Hampered by his outsider status, Hawkins struggled to build relationships with the burgeoning modern dance institutions. And to make matters worse, the poor press he received in the late 1940s continued, with few exceptions, into the early 1950s.

The most positive press Hawkins received in the 1950s was from a surprising source, Louis Horst. Overcoming the complications of the 1938 love triangle between himself, Graham, and Hawkins,

Horst reviewed the premiere of Hawkins' *Here and Now with Watchers* writing,

> Mr. Hawkins has apparently embraced the art philosophies of avant-garde-ism. And, truth to tell, he seems to function in this area much more successfully than many others of this aesthetic attitude … *Here and Now with Watchers* was superbly performed with dignity, taste and sincere belief.[14]

It had been five years since Hawkins presented a dance, putting his place in the genre, as well as his artistic direction into question. The considerable influence of Horst's review did much to legitimize Hawkins' re-entry into the field and acted as an endorsement of Hawkins' position as an avant-garde artist. Hawkins comments, "Louis [Horst] came around! Louis had a lot of guts. He was our biggest champion for *Here and Now with Watchers*. He wrote the first reviews. And changed everything and he stuck up for me."[15]

In addition to the work that Horst's review did to launch the next phase of Hawkins' career, the placement of the review within the January 1958 edition of *Dance Observer* offers an analogy to Hawkins' place in the genre. Horst's review was one of several other reviews on emerging and mid-tier choreographers that appeared in the middle of the journal. In contrast, the cover of that issue featured a photo of Cunningham with Viola Farber in Cunningham's *Nocturnes* (1956). These locations in the *Dance Observer* reveal Hawkins and Cunningham's location in the field of modern dance at the time. By the end of the 1950s, Cunningham had become a prominent figure within the field, while Hawkins was emerging—again.

Cunningham joined the Martha Graham Dance Company in 1939, a year after Hawkins, and left in 1945. From *Every Soul is a Circus* (1939) to *Appalachian Spring* (1944), Cunningham and Hawkins were the featured men in the cast. Cunningham presented his first independent work in 1944, which was the first in a series of life-long collaborations with John Cage. When Cunningham left the Graham Company in 1945, he had already established his collaborative partnership with Cage, both professionally and romantically and together they had begun developing a group of core collaborators that would include the visual and multi-media artists, Robert Rauschenberg and Jasper Johns. It was clear by the mid-to-late 1940s that Cunningham had abandoned Graham's expressionist traditions and was not looking back. Conversely, from 1945 until Hawkins left the Graham Company in 1950, Hawkins choreographed four dances, all of which were literary-based and presented in the expressionistic style of Graham. And compared to Cunningham's relatively smooth transition out of the Graham Company, Hawkins' exit left him ostracized from the Graham circle, physically injured, and without artistic collaborators. Charting a new direction within this context would be extremely difficult, but his circumstances shifted when he met Lucia Dlugoszewski.

Lucia Dlugoszewski

Dlugoszewski was born in Detroit, Michigan in 1925 and died in New York City in 2000.[16] She moved to New York in 1949 to study Bach with Grete Sultan and music analysis with Felix Salzer. Dlugoszewski met Hawkins in 1951 through her Bach instructor Sultan. Sultan's studio was next to Hawkins' and when Hawkins asked him to recommend a piano accompanist who could also compose, Sultan recommended Dlugoszewski. Dlugoszewski and Hawkins began a professional and romantic relationship that continued for the remainder of their lives. They married on September 1, 1962, but kept it private. Dlugoszewski writes, "Because of professional choice, it was only after 1994 that I for the first time publicly faced the world as Erick's wife."[17]

In 1951 Dlugoszewski began experimenting with what she called the "timbre piano," an instrument and process that involved modifying the sounds of the piano, as well as the pianist's engagement with it. She did this by adding everyday objects to the piano's strings and giving the pianist unorthodox instructions for touching, hammering, and plucking the piano. This, of course, was not new. In 1923, Henry Cowell began composing pieces in which pianists interacted with the piano strings in unconventional ways and in 1940 John Cage began work on his "prepared piano," in which he modified or added objects to the piano and its strings. Composer Hal Rammel writes that Dlugoszewski's timbre piano differed from her predecessor's through her approach to "the piano more as an extended string orchestra than as the two-handed percussion ensemble."[18] The creation of her timbre piano at this early stage of her career was not only significant because it put her in dialogue with leading vanguard artists, but it also became foundational in establishing her career-long focus on timbre, tonal quality, and color.[19]

In 1951, Dlugoszewski began studying composition with Edgard
Varése. At the time, Varése and Cage, were leading the way in two
divergent and oppositional compositional approaches: timbre and
rhythm for Varése and chance operations for Cage. It is unclear if
Dlugoszewski's choice to follow Varése rather than Cage was influenced by Hawkins' competition with Cunningham, but what is clear
is that her choice distanced the Dlugoszewski/Hawkins' avant-garde
project from what would become the more widely acknowledged
and predominant Cage/Cunningham/Judson avant-garde scene.

Beginning with, *Space is a Diamond* (1970), her composition for
trumpet virtuoso Gerard Schwarz, Dlugoszewski's work gained
recognition beyond the dance scene and smaller avant-garde circles.
In 1971, she received two commissions from the prominent group,
American Brass Quintet.[20] The success of these two pieces was followed by more commissions and recognition. Her *Abyss and Caress*
(1975) was commissioned by the National Endowment for the Arts
in conjunction with the New York Philharmonic. Its first performance was a prestigious affair, conducted by the renowned conductor, Pierre Boulez. In 1977 she became the first woman to receive
the Koussevitzky International Recording Award for *Fire Fragile
Flight* (1973), which was recorded for Candide by Joel Thome's
Orchestra of Our Time.

Dlugoszewski and Hawkins

Dlugoszewski was still an emerging avant-garde artist when she met
Hawkins, who was approximately 15 years her senior and already an
established artist. While this context set up Dlugoszewski as
Hawkins' mentee, her influence on Hawkins' work cannot be overlooked. Nor can the likelihood that her influence on him received
little or no recognition. When Dlugoszewski and Hawkins met in
1951, Dlugoszewski's interest in avant-garde experimentation was far
removed from the more traditional work Hawkins had done with
Ballet Caravan and the Graham Company. From the time she
arrived in New York in 1949, Dlugoszewski had cultivated associations with avant-garde circles and created experimental compositions that incorporated everyday objects played in non-traditional
spaces. Her collaborations with vanguard artists and associations with
avant-garde communities presented new possibilities and directions
for Hawkins. Notably, Dlugoszewski facilitated Hawkins' connection to multi-media artist, Ralph Dorazio. Dlugoszewski and

Dorazio had met in the mid-1940s while students at Wayne State University in Detroit, Michigan. They married, but divorced before separately moving to New York to continue their careers.[21] Dorazio became a core collaborators of Hawkins' and worked with him, as well as Dlugoszewski throughout their careers.

Beginning with *openings of the (eye)* (1952), Dlugoszewski wrote the music for nearly all of Hawkins' dances from 1952 to 1971.[22] Her music for *openings of the (eye)*, was the premiere performance of her timbre piano and also included flute and percussion. She worked with Dorazio on the design and construction of the percussion instruments used in the piece. She also performed the piece onstage, while Hawkins danced, which would become a common practice for them. Allen Hughes' review of *Of Love* (1971) provides an example of the staging, "she [Dlugoszewski] will very likely move with the studied control of a dancer, sitting or kneeling in front of a Helen Frankenthaler banner painting, playing her unique percussion instruments."[23]

Increasingly drawn to percussive instruments, Dlugoszewski began work on a new piece in 1957 for which she and Dorazio designed and built over 100 percussion instruments. These included a variety of rattles, square-shaped drums, gongs, and ladder harps, many of which were made from non-traditional materials such as paper, glass, plastic, and metal. Dlugoszewski referred to these instruments as an orchestra and used them as a score for Hawkins' *8 Clear Places* as well as for her *Suchness Concert* (1958). She writes, "in 1958, when Erick created *8 Clear Places*, I felt I should not write music in which my piddling emotions would interfere with the dance. That's when I began to invent percussion instruments."[24]

Rather than the traditional approach to a dancer's embodiment of music, Dlugoszewski and Hawkins sought to present music and dance as distinct compositional elements. Dlugoszewski explains, "the dances came first. I'd watch rehearsals and analyze the dance from the point of view of time, energy, dynamic levels and poetry."[25] Dlugoszewski argued that neither her music nor Hawkins' choreography would be superimposed on the other. She writes that sound, "has the power to hold its own against the charms of the most beautiful body because *it has the same power as a beautiful body*."[26] Dlugoszewski proposes that music is more than a mere background, it is a visceral theatrical event that audience members can use to experience their embodied participation. She writes that when we really listen, we:

discover that our ears are on either side of the head ... that music is the making and hearing of a sound—is thus a form of theatre, really the most exquisite of theatres. Juxtaposition is another delight. Dance is another theatre.[27]

In 1968, at the urging of Hawkins, Dlugoszewski began teaching composition classes for the Hawkins Company. Composer and accompanist Eleanor Hovda, who worked and studied in both the Cunningham and Hawkins studios, recalls:

> She [Dlugoszewski] and Erick would teach June courses every year ... Lucia would teach composition to the dancers, and Erick would teach dance. It would be a very concentrated 3- or 4-week session. I took one of those, and I just thought it was wonderful. I took Erick's classes, and I took Lucia's composition class, and it was a really interesting kind of thing, because the two of them were so interconnected that you really didn't think of one as distinct from the other.[28]

Dlugoszewski assumed Artistic Directorship of the Erick Hawkins Dance Company in 1996, two years after Hawkins passed away. Her first choreographic project was to complete three dances Hawkins had begun outlining in his choreographic notebook. The first one completed, *Journey of a Poet*, was performed by White Oak Dance Project in 1997. The other two, *Why Does a Man Dance?* and *Last Love Duet* were presented in the Hawkins Company's 1999 season at the 92nd Street Y. Dlugoszewski's first solo choreographic output, *Radical Ardent*, was also presented in this concert, receiving mixed reviews. Dlugoszewski's death in 2000 was unexpected. She died on the Tuesday of a show week in which the Hawkins Company was presenting her newest dance, *Motherwell Amor*, dedicated to her friend, the painter Robert Motherwell. She had no will or heirs. And to complicate the matter, when Hawkins passed away in 1994, he had left his estate to her, which further clouded their legacies as both collaborators and individual artists.

Challenges and erasures

One is hard-pressed to think of another female composer writing for modern dance during the span of Dlugoszewski's career. Beginning with the Godfather of modern dance composers, Louis Horst, the field was dominated by men, such as Norman Lloyd, Wallinford Riegger, Carlos Surinach, Norman Dello Joio, John Cage, and David Diamond. In "Composer/Choreographer," *Dance Perspectives'* 1963 summary of 11 modern dance composers, Vivian Fine and Dlugoszewski are the only women included.[29] Not only was the field dominated by men, but these men were able to move easily between composing for musicians and composing for choreographers. They also moved among choreographers, composing for more than one choreographer. Dlugoszewski's movement between disciplines was difficult and she composed for no other choreographer than Hawkins.

Dlugoszewski's position in the field was further complicated by her limited record of published scores and opposition to trending ideas in modern music. Dlugoszewski did not publish many of her scores, which diminished her standing, perhaps as a way for the Hawkins Dance Company to avoid financial negotiations with music publishers.[30] And her rejection of chance operations and serial methods added to the unequal and biased treatment of her and her music. Although Dlugoszewski did ultimately receive recognition for her work it was regularly gendered, as in the headline of Robert Crowley's review of her work, "Percussion Music Created, Played in Tour De Force by Lady Musician." Although Crowley's article praised Dlugoszewski as a trailblazing composer and performer, he contextualizes her within a title that replaces her name with a gender.[31]

Dlugoszewski's disenfranchisement from the Cage circle, paired with Hawkins' excommunication from the Graham circle, left the Dlugoszewski/Hawkins project with a limited number of allies. Hovda opines on Dlugoszewski and Hawkins' position in their fields:

> She [Dlugoszewski] didn't just sort of fit naturally into the composing world like a lot of people do; she was respected by a lot of people and hated by others. I mean, this evidently was par for the course, but she and Erick were convinced that the world was against them. They were absolutely convinced of this. They might have been too early for their time.[32]

Yes, perhaps too early and perhaps too catholic in their tastes. It is interesting to examine the Hawkins/Dlugoszewski project through their merging of postwar avant-garde and prewar expressionist aesthetics. By merging postwar experimental techniques of composition and embodiment with prewar expressionist aesthetics Hawkins and Dlugoszewski created an incongruous fusion that was difficult for both avant-gardists and expressionists to grasp. Although Hawkins and Dlugoszewski's approaches to composition and embodiment were radical breaks from prewar expressionistic conventions, their career-long exploration of "nature" and "natural bodies" was steeped in traditional notions of harmony and wholeness that ran counter to more prominent avant-garde notions of randomness or everydayness. In "Erick Hawkins: Heir to a New Tradition," Dlugoszewski discusses her and Hawkins' relationship with their avant-garde colleagues. She writes:

> the deep naturalness of Erick Hawkins' highly trained dancing is different from the new "non-dance"—that avant-garde pursuit of untrained, utilitarian human movement. Hawkins' naturalness always has the quickening interest and living freshness of something in nature. On the other hand, the avant-garde, every-day-life movement imitating performance of tasks or work in its very different "naturalism" has exhibited in the theatre over and over again a curious seemingly unavoidable dullness.[33]

Dlugoszewski's use of technique and training to differentiate Hawkins from Judson-based dancers was a central tactic they used throughout their careers to position their work as high art. Like the Humphrey/Limón project, Dlugoszewski and Hawkins remained embedded within divisions between high and low art and the sanctity of performance as ritual from the everyday or popular.

Techniques

Marcel Mauss' 1934 piece, *Techniques of the Body*, was one of the earliest texts to theorize how the movements, actions, and gestures of people were developed co-constitutively with their culture. Mauss forwards the term "techniques" as actions that are "effective and traditional. There is no technique and no transmission in the absence of tradition."[34] My interest in Mauss' work lies in how this notion of tradition is comprised of repetition and habit and how one acquires the appropriate and efficient techniques to move within a culture. While Mauss' work has been expounded on by many scholars, I'm particularly interested in Susan Foster's discussion of repetition and the creation of habits in dance. Foster theorizes the repetition that takes place in technical training as a ceaseless drilling, a need to continuously repeat movement in order to master them. She writes "the aim is nothing less than *creating the body*."[35] Through repetition, metaphors used for training become concrete; they become embodied, until over many years, the body is reconfigured, remade. While repetition is necessary to make particular movements "second nature," repetition is also the primary cause for dance injuries. Executing exercises repeatedly, if done without care, can cause undue stress that can lead to injury. In similar ways, the repetition of the cultural narratives embedded within a dancer's technical training can also cause stress to the social body that lead to injury. Recognizing the internalization of these cultural narratives and performing them in self-reflective ways offers ways to prevent injury and help heal the social body.

Like their predecessors, Hawkins and Limón developed their particular techniques through a specific approach to the physical laws of movement, or "movement principles" such as alignment, distribution of weight, relationship to gravity, turnout, sequential movement of the torso, etc. And while both Hawkins and Limón's techniques, styles, and choreography used abstract and formalist conventions that only obliquely engaged social concerns, their movement techniques and performing styles were symbiotically entwined with their respective geo-political spaces: Hawkins' Euro-American heritage and Limón's Mexican-American heritage. As such, their techniques are inseparable from the socio-political privileges and freedoms that each choreographer used to develop their style.

From Shawn to Hawkins

It was Shawn, more so than St. Denis, who trained dancers at Denishawn. And the majority of the training consisted of ballet and Delsarte-based "movement studies." Shawn's own studies began with ballet at the age of 19 in Denver, Colorado, as part of his recovery program from a bout of diphtheria. His study of The Delsarte Method began in 1915, with Henrietta Hovey. It was a time when the Delsarte Method was primarily used to acquire the skills of articulation, diction, enunciation, and vocalization. Skills that would distinguish the student as sophisticated and refined, thereby increasing their cultural capital. And although Shawn led the way in adapting the Delsarte Method for modern dance, he did little to modify the Delsarte Method's notion of self-expression which focused on the ability to express an external text, rather than an individual's particular experience of being in the world.

As former students of Shawn and St. Denis, Graham and Humphrey's early work from the late 1920s drew on the choreographic approaches and cultural references established by Denishawn. However, they were developing new modes of self-expression that abandoned Denishawn's values. Rather than performing as a Delsartean/Denishawnian interpretive intermediary between the text and audience, Graham and Humphrey developed a notion of self-expression that would merge their personal and particular experience of being in the world with timeless and universal "truths." Such an innovation required radical new movement vocabularies and creating them was Graham and Humphrey's first and most important task. The idea of developing a technique or training regime, as we know it today, was a by-product of this work. It was from Graham and Humphrey's personal movement vocabularies, built on their particular proclivities and strengths as movers, that their techniques and training regimes would slowly emerge.

The primary need for Graham and Humphrey to construct and codify a technique and training program was to efficiently transmit their personal styles onto dancers, create stylistically cohesive group works, and develop schools. These needs and processes were not unique to Graham or Humphrey, it was the common practice for choreographers across genres. There seemed to be no other reason or way a choreographer would do otherwise. The convention of the time placed the choreographer as Artistic Director from whom a singular stylistic, philosophical, and artistic vision was passed down to dancers and audiences.

Hawkins modified this process, which is key to appreciating his interventions. When Hawkins left Graham and her company, both parties were bearing physical and emotional injuries. The knee and back injuries that Hawkins sustained played a significant role in spurring his pursuit of a more holistic and anatomically conscientious approach to training and performing. In the early 1950s Hawkins discovered Mabel Todd's *The Thinking Body* which proved to be foundational for his new work. Through his study of Todd's writings, as well as the practices of her mentees, Barbara Clark, and Lulu Sweigard, Hawkins developed a method of training that focused on reeducating neuromuscular processes through the power of imagination. What has come to be known as ideokinesis.[36] The choreographic style that Hawkins would develop from this approach was a radical departure from the expressionism practiced by his predecessors. He argued that his technique and style was not developed from his personal movement proclivities and egotistical needs as he proposed Graham had done, but rather on the objective findings of "anatomical science." Hawkins recalls,

> Through my own injuries I began to see what the science of kinesiology was finding out about movement and dance technique … So, I began to see that we could not have a new dance in America if we based our movement on anything that violated science.[37]

Hawkins' approach was a radical move that catalyzed a new branch of dance research, a move that many feel has gone unrecognized. In his book, *The Body is a Clear Place*, Hawkins made his claim:

> kinesiology is the science, what can be known and verified by all knowers, the theoretical component. On this level, I was the pioneer and the only one, so far as I know, to have succeeded in using these verifiable kinesiological principles in the teaching of dance technique and in the framework of a practicing dancer and significant, meaningful artist/choreographer.[38]

And not only was Hawkins pivotal in introducing kinesiology to dance, but he also mentored future leaders in the somatic and kinesiological field, including Bonnie Bainbridge Cohen and André Bernard.

Universal science

Hawkins' kinesiological approach to movement complicated conventional approaches to embodiment and offered new ways for dancers to perform universal themes. In the 1978 Erick Hawkins School Brochure, in a section titled, "On the Hawkins Technique" Hawkins writes,

> the first requirement of a correct dance training is, therefore, to train the novice only in the brightest, ascertainable, correct laws of moving according to scientific principles, that is according to

nature ... The laws would be as true for a Hottentot, a New Yorker, or a citizen of Peking.[39]

Hawkins' discussion of universality under the auspices of science intervened in modern dance's existing conventions for performing a universal body. These conventions were based on a transformative process that merged a dancer's personal identity with "timeless truths." For Hawkins, this transformative process was an imposition on the already universal functioning of the human body. His project focused on expressing universal themes through the materiality of the dancing body as it moved through time and space. There was no need to use emotions, psychological states, or story as a transformative vehicle.

And although Hawkins' scientific contextualization of universality intervened in predominant expressionistic conventions, it was not new. Shawn had made such a move in his 1954 book, the full title of which makes his focus on "science" clear, *Every Little Movement; A Book About François Delsarte, The Man and His Philosophy, His Science of Applied Aesthetics, The Application of This Science to the Art of the Dance, The Influence of Delsarte on American Dance.* Shawn's thesis is that Delsarte's scientific work had been diluted by ill-informed practitioners who "made ridiculous what was then, and is now, the most complete and perfect science of human expression."[40] Shawn claimed that his book would recover the "true" science on which Delsarte based his work, which would bring credibility to Delsarte, his own work, and the genre of modern dance.

Delsarte developed his theories in the mid-nineteenth-century, when science was replacing religion as the dominant producer and arbiter of knowledge. It was an uneven replacement complicated by the simultaneous rise of what we now refer to as the pseudo-sciences, some of which Delsarte incorporated into his work. For example, Delsarte's work was deeply influenced by the writings of the eighteenth-century moral philosopher and physiognomist, Johann Caspar Lavater. Delsarte drew on Lavater's work to develop his foundational theory of three "body zones" that performers could draw on to express themselves.[41] Delsarte also subscribed to other pseudo-sciences, such as phrenology and mesmerism, subscriptions that would ultimately lead to the abandonment of his work.[42] However, before it was abandoned, Delsarte was highly respected and the Delsarte Method was all the rage. From 1870 to 1900, it was the leading program for actor training in the United States and inspired many adaptations that, as Shawn argued, moved far afield from the "true" Delsartean "science."

Hawkins' integration of scientific principles into his work was contextualized within this nineteenth-century scientific community that helped establish hierarchies of race, gender, and class within which twentieth-century choreographers worked. During Hawkins' career, the hierarchies of race embedded within this scientific community were slowly fading, but still influential. Since the over-whelming majority of scientists in the nineteenth and early-twentieth-century were Euro-American men, the objectivity of science became grafted onto white male bodies. And this objectivity was used to legitimize scientific inquiry and social practices that assessed and dif-ferentiated bodies. As American historian, Sander Gilman argues, the objectivity and value-neutral status accorded to science is made at the cost of erasing its social, historical, and sociological context.[43] After all, science is a social activity and its claim to knowledge must be examined for the social context and the particular social position of the one making the claim. Using the purported objectivity of science to create categorizations of diversity, or in Hawkins' case, categorizations of universality, is a fraught enterprise.

The Hawkins style

By making kinesiological principles an important part of his tech-nique, Hawkins developed a style that was unlike anything modern dance audiences had seen. Compared to the predominant styles of Limón and Graham who used tension-based "bound-flow" move-ment, Hawkins' style felt "released." Hawkins transferred his released style onto his dancers by training them to "sense" their bodies as sources of information in time and space. Former Hawkins Company dancer Nada Diachenko comments, "he always recom-mended that we all study that [ideokinesis]. André Bernard was ... a wonderful teacher of Mabel Todd's work.[44] And Erick would always advise people to study on the outside, so you could go deeper."[45] The resulting style asked audiences, who were accustomed to Limón and Graham's performance of effort and tension, to find new ways to connect with the Hawkins dancers as they "sensed" the easeful flow of their bodies in time and space. Given the Hawkins' dancers facile and released movements, it appeared to many viewers that they were not working as hard as the Graham or Limón dancers. While some audience members appreciated the beauty of Hawkins' dancers as they focused on "sensing" their bodies, others could only see self-absorbed dancers not interested in communicating with them. Deborah Jowitt articulates the reception of the Hawkins Company, "It is perhaps this quality of making their own sensations manifest that makes them appear so beautifully and innocently hedonistic to some viewers and so self-centered to others."[46]

Hawkins' approach to choreographing for groups of dancers also perplexed modern dance audiences. As discussed earlier, Hawkins' dances throughout the 1950s were solos or duets, a decade when Limón and Graham were developing new and more complex ways to move groups of dancers around the stage. So, when Hawkins began producing group works in the 1960s, audiences had developed certain expectations per Limón, Graham, and their contemporaries. For example, Limón seamlessly moved large groups of dancers on and off stage; created various voicings between dancers; and multiple levels within groups. And while Limón's groupings had a completeness all their own, he regularly used them as a background, transition, or foil to dramatize his own highly charged solos and duets that became the central focus of the dance. Conversely, Hawkins' choreography regularly featured groups that moved in unison and made simple geometric floor patterns. And rather than using a corps of dancers as a background for solos and duets, Hawkins' used the corps as the main event. Hawkins replaced the relationship between soloist and group with a relationship between a group of humans and the "natural" world.

Many of Hawkins' most staunch supporters began as harsh critics. For example, dance writer Robert Sabin, who disparaged Hawkins' choreography in the early 1950s, came to support his work and defended his "effortless" style of dance. Sabin writes:

> Hawkins' work has one disturbing confrontation for all of us, revealing how subtly puritanical we are in our basic fear of effortlessness ... Whether it is disguised effort or dramatized effort or outer-oriented effort, all these other techniques in no way conflict with our past cultural psychology. But a discipline of effortlessness is something else again, and a certain amount of psychological resistance to it can be expected.[47]

As Sabin writes, the relationship between choreography and a puritanical work ethic that audiences had internalized was not a new postwar phenomenon invented to disparage Hawkins' dancers. It had been integral in prewar modern dance as choreographers sought to differentiate modern dance from "ethnic" dance and entertainment. The effort, labor, and discipline attributed to modern dance techniques were contrasted with the "freedom," release, and effortlessness of "ethnic," non-Western, or indigenous dancers whose movement, it was argued, required little or no technique. It was assumed that without the need for control, discipline, or labor, "ethnic" or indigenous dancers did not require a technique, they could simply release their bodies and move freely.

By using technique to differentiate between modern dance and non-Western cultures, Graham's generation of expressionistic dancers constructed a dichotomy through which Euro-American choreographers could manage notions of primitivism and indigeneity as vehicles to perform "natural," primitive, and pre-industrial bodies. Although Hawkins participated in this practice while with the Graham Company, his integration of kinesiological principles after he left intervened in expressionistic conventions. However, his work still left the dichotomies used to differentiate between technically trained white bodies and "untrained" non-white bodies in place.

Conclusion

Many of Hawkins' dances opened on an empty stage with no audio and a blue cyclorama. He regularly paused on this blue emptiness, offering audiences a comparatively long time to tune in and be aware of how they were listening and seeing, an opportunity to "be here now." This use of temporality was an important aspect of his avant-garde project. He writes, "when the immediacy and pure existence of movement is the prime concern, time is a much more serious problem of dance than space. Time is also a much richer material of dance than space."[48] Presenting, sharing, and performing time in this radical way was not a practice that was quickly and widely appreciated. Audiences were more accustomed to traditional uses of time as an element in dramatic narratives that moved a presentation along. Nevertheless, Hawkins preserved. His commitment to his work inspired his collaborators and dancers and offered powerful new approaches to embodiment, technique, and performance.

Notes

1 Prevots, Naomi. "Erick Hawkins: Redefining America." In 7 Essays on the Dance of Erick Hawkins. Kisselgoff, Anna et al New York; Foundation for Modern Dance. 1982.
2 When asked whether he took Horst's classes, Hawkins replied "Yes, I took it once." Interview by David Sears. May 27, 1983.
3 Horst Interview, 1952.
4 Horst Interview, 1952.
5 Horst Interview, 1952.
6 Horst quoted in Soares, Janet Mansfield. Louis Horst: Musician in a Dancers World. Durham, NC: Duke University Press, 1992.
7 Erick Hawkins, Poet of the Modern Dance—Speaking of Dance. Dir. Douglas Rosenberg. 1995.
8 Limón, José. "An American Accent." In The Modern Dance: Seven Statements of Belief, edited by Selma Jeanne Cohen. Middletown, CT: Wesleyan University Press. 1966: 17–27, 23.
9 Hawkins, Erick. Interview by David Sears. May 27, 1983.
10 Trickster Coyote was revived in 1965 and again in 1983. John Brown was based on the Kansan abolitionist of the same name. The cast consisted of Hawkins as John Brown and an interlocutor reciting text written by Hawkins. It was developed from Freestater Kansas, the third of four sections in an earlier solo called, Liberty Tree (1941). In yet another iteration of the abolitionist, Hawkins transformed John Brown into God's Angry Man in 1965 and made even more revisions to it again in 1985.
11 Johnston, Jill. Marmalade Me. New York: Dutton, 1971.
12 Erdman, Jean. Interview by Linda Small. December 21, 1978.
13 Hawkins, Erick. Interview by David Sears. June 9, 1985.
14 Horst, Louis. "Here and Now with Watchers." Dance Observer. January 1958.
15 Hawkins, Erick. Interview by Don McDonagh. November 17, 1972.
16 Dlugoszewski's actual birth date is unknown. Dates range from 1925 to 1934.
17 Celichowska, Renata. The Erick Hawkins Modern Dance Technique. N.J. Princeton Book Company, 2000.
18 Rammel, Hal. Dlugoszewski, Lucia. Disparate Stairway, Radical Other. 1978. CD.
19 Dlugoszewski's compositions from this period include: Transparencies 1–50 for Everyday Sounds (1951), Everyday Sounds for Bright by E.E. Cummings (1951), and Orchestra Structure for the Poetry of Everyday Sounds (1952). She also composed an incidental score for The Living Theatre's production of Alfred Jarry's play Ubu Roi in 1952.
20 Hawkins used these scores for Angels of the Inmost Heaven (1971) and Of Love (1971).
21 Dlugoszewski performed her composition, Structures for the Poetry of Everyday Sounds (1952) in the loft of sculptor, Ralph Dorazio.
22 The dances that Dlugoszewski did not write for were: Bridegroom of the Moon (1952) by Wallingford Riegger and Lives of Five or Six Swords (1952) and Naked Leopard (1965) both by Lou Harrison. After 1970,

Dlugoszewski received an increasing number of commissions, which inhibited her from maintaining a consistent collaborative input into Hawkins' dances.

23 Hughes, Allen. "And Miss Dlugoszewski Experiments—A Lot," *New York Times*, March 1971.

24 Dlugoszewski quoted in Rammel, Hal. Dlugoszewski, Lucia. *Disparate Stairway, Radical Other*. 1978. CD.

25 Dunning, Jennifer. "The Composer who Energizes the Erick Hawkins Dancers." *New York Times*. December 7, 1988.

26 Dlugoszewski quoted in Cohen, Selma Jean and A.J. Pischl. "Composer/Choreographer." *Dance Perspectives 16*. 1963: pp. 3–61. Italics in original.

27 Dlugoszewski quoted in Cohen, Selma Jean and A.J. Pischl. "Composer/Choreographer." *Dance Perspectives 16*. 1963: pp. 3–61. Italics in original.

28 Hovda quoted in Blackburn, Philip. *The American Composers Forum for American Public Media*. "Eleanor Hovda remembers Lucia Dlugoszewski." http://musicmavericks.publicradio.org/features/interview_dluguszewskil. May 2003. February 2019.

29 Vivian Fine wrote for Charles Weidman, Hanya Holm, and Martha Graham.

30 Doyle, Kate. "Discovering Creative Connections: The Collaboration of Erick Hawkins and Lucia Dlugoszewski." *Library of Congress*. Uploaded by James Moreno. April 11, 2017. www.loc.gov/item/webcast-8138. January 20, 2019.

31 Robert Crowley, Portland Reporter. 1962. 63.

32 Hovda quoted in Blackburn, Philip. *The American Composers Forum for American Public Media*. "Eleanor Hovda remembers Lucia Dlugoszewski." http://musicmavericks.publicradio.org/features/interview_dluguszewskil. May 2003. February 2019.

33 Dlugoszewski, Lucia. "Erick Hawkins: Heir to a New Tradition." In *5 Essays on the Dance of Erick Hawkins*, edited by M.L. Gordon Norton. New York: Foundation for Modern Dance. 1973: 26–39. 32.

34 Mauss, Marcel. "Techniques of the Body." *Economy and Society* 2. 1973: 70–88. 75.

35 Foster, Susan Leigh. "Dancing Bodies." In *Meaning in Motion: New Cultural Studies of Dance*, edited by Jane Desmond. Durham, NC: Duke University Press, 1997.

36 André Bernard writes,

> The label *ideokinesis* was coined by the American piano teacher Bonpensière, who was popular in the 1920s and 1920s … Sweigard borrowed the word from Bonpensière to describe her methodology. Ideokinesis can be translated roughly as "the image or thought as facilitator of the movement." Ideokinesis began to be used as a label for the work after the publication in 1974 of Sweigard's book *Human Movement Potential*, in which she used the work.
>
> (Bernard, *Ideokinesis* 5)

37 Myers quoted in Celichowska, Renata. *The Erick Hawkins Modern Dance Technique.* 2000.
38 Hawkins, Erick. *The Body Is a Clear Place and Other Statements on Dance.* 1992. 95.
39 Hawkins quoted in Celichowska, Renata. *The Erick Hawkins Modern Dance Technique.* 2000.
40 Shawn, Ted. *Every Little Movement: A Book about François Delsarte, the Man and His Philosophy, His Science of Applied Aesthetics, the Application of This Science to the Art of the Dance, the Influence of Delsarte on American Dance.* Dance Horizons/Princeton Book Co., 1954.
41 Shawn, Ted. *Every Little Movement: A Book about François Delsarte, the Man and His Philosophy, His Science of Applied Aesthetics, the Application of This Science to the Art of the Dance, the Influence of Delsarte on American Dance.* Dance Horizons/Princeton Book Co., 1954.
42 Walker, Julia. *Expressionism and Modernism in the American Theatre: Bodies, Voices, Words.* Cambridge University Press, 2009.
43 Gilman, Sander. "Black Bodies, White Bodies: Toward an Iconography of Female Sexuality in Late Nineteenth-Century Art, Medicine, and Literature." *Critical Inquiry.* Vol. 12, No. 1, "Race," Writing, and Difference. Autumn. 1985: 204–242. 205.
44 Bernard refers to his work as "a creative approach to human movement and alignment" (Bernard, 9). Although Sweigard's term, ideokinesis, has become the predominate term for this work Bernard contributed the term, "physiophilosophy." He argues that, "as much as anything, this is a philosophy of the body and how you relate to it" (Bernard, 9). Bernard, André, et al. *Ideokinesis: A Creative Approach to Human Movement and Body Alignment.* Berkeley, CA: North Atlantic Books, 2006.
45 Diachenko, Nada. Interview by Caroline Sutton Clark. January 8, 2010.
46 Jowitt, Deborah. "Review." *The Village Voice.* September 1981.
47 Sabin, Robert. "What Comes After the Avant-Garde." In *5 Essays on the Dance of Erick Hawkins,* edited by M.L. Gordon Norton. New York: Foundation for Modern Dance. 1973: 40–57.
48 Hawkins quoted in Olinsky, Lillian. "The Uncommunicating Choreography of Erick Hawkins." *Dance Magazine.* March 1959: 3–85. 45 and 8.

Works cited

Bernard, André, Wolfgang Steinmüller and Ursula Stricker. *Ideokinesis: A Creative Approach to Human Movement and Body Alignment.* Berkeley, CA: North Atlantic Books, 2006.
Celichowska, Renata. *The Erick Hawkins Modern Dance Technique.* Hightstown, NJ: Princeton Book Co. 2000.
Cohen, Selma Jean and A.J. Pischl. "Composer/Choreographer." *Dance Perspectives* 16. 1963: 3–61.
Crowley, Robert. Portland Reporter, 1962: 63.
Diachenko, Nada. Interview by Caroline Sutton Clark. January 8, 2010.
Doyle, Kate. "Discovering Creative Connections: The Collaboration of Erick Hawkins and Lucia Dlugoszewski." Library of Congress. Uploaded

by James Moreno. April 11, 2017. www.loc.gov/item/webcast-8138. January 20, 2019.

Dunning, Jennifer. "The Composer who Energizes the Erick Hawkins Dancers." *New York Times*. December 7, 1988.

Erdman, Jean. Interview by Linda Small. December 21, 1978.

Foster, Susan Leigh. "Dancing Bodies." In *Meaning in Motion: New Cultural Studies of Dance*, edited by Jane Desmond. Durham, NC: Duke University Press, 1997.

Gilman, Sander. "Black Bodies, White Bodies: Toward an Iconography of Female Sexuality in Late Nineteenth-Century Art, Medicine, and Literature." *Critical Inquiry*. Vol. 12, No. 1, "Race," *Writing, and Difference*. Autumn. 1985: 204–242. 205.

Hawkins, Erick. Interview by Don McDonagh. November 17, 1972.

Hawkins, Erick. Interview by David Sears. May 27, 1983.

Hawkins, Erick. Interview by David Sears. June 9, 1985.

Hawkins, Erick. *The Body Is a Clear Place and Other Statements on Dance*. Pennington, NJ: Dance Horizons/Princeton Book Co. 1992.

Hawkins, Erick. Poet of the Modern Dance—Speaking of Dance. Dir. Douglas Rosenberg. 1995.

Horst, Louis. "Here and Now with Watchers." *Dance Observer*. January 1958.

Horst, Louis. Interview. 1952.

Horst quoted in Soares, Janet Mansfield. *Louis Horst: Musician in a Dancers World*. Durham, NC: Duke University Press, 1992.

Hovda quoted in Blackburn, Philip. The American Composers Forum for American Public Media. "Eleanor Hovda remembers Lucia Dlugoszwski." http://musicmavericks.publicradio.org/features/interview_dluguszewskil. May 2003. February 2019.

Hughes, Allen. "And Miss Dlugoszewski Experiments—A Lot." *New York Times*. March 1971.

Johnston, Jill. *Marmalade Me*. New York: Dutton, 1971.

Jowitt, Deborah. "Review." *The Village Voice*. September 1981.

Limón, José. "An American Accent." In *The Modern Dance: Seven Statements of Belief*, edited by Selma Jeanne Cohen. Middletown, CT: Wesleyan University Press. 1966: 17–27.

Mauss, Marcel. "Techniques of the Body." *Economy and Society* 2. 1973: 70–88. 75.

Olinsky, Lillian. "The Uncommunicating Choreography of Erick Hawkins." *Dance Magazine*. March 1959: 3–85.

Prevots, Naomi. "Erick Hawkins: Redefining America." In *7 Essays on the Dance of Erick Hawkins*. Kisselgoff, Anna et al. New York: Foundation for Modern Dance. 1982.

Rammel, Hal. Dlugoszewski, Lucia. *Disparate Stairway, Radical Other*. 1978. CD.

Sabin, Robert. "What Comes After the Avant-Garde." In *5 Essays on the Dance of Erick Hawkins*, edited by M.L. Gordon Norton. New York: Foundation for Modern Dance, 1973: 40–57.

Shawn, Ted. *Every Little Movement: A Book about François Delsarte, the Man and His Philosophy, His Science of Applied Aesthetics, the Application of This Science to the Art of the Dance, the Influence of Delsarte on American Dance.* Pennington, NJ: Dance Horizons/Princeton Book Co., 1954.

Soares, Janet Mansfield. *Louis Horst: Musician in a Dancers World.* Durham, NC: Duke University Press, 1992.

Walker, Julia. *Expressionism and Modernism in the American Theatre: Bodies, Voices, Words.* New York: Cambridge University Press, 2009.

Chapter 2

Limón's biblical dances

Introduction

In 1942 Doris Humphrey invited Limón to compose a dance for an all-Bach program she was producing in her 14th St Studio Theatre. Limón accepted and began working on a piece he would title *Chaconne*, set to the chaconne from J.S. Bach's Partita in D minor for solo violin. As part of his choreographic process, Limón workshopped an early version for Humphrey, who, after watching it commented, "this is one of the most magnificent dances I have ever seen. It is that for a number of reasons, but chiefly because it is a man dancing."[1] Why the spectacle of the male dancing body is magnificent, as well as offensive, eroticized, dissident, and complicit is the subject of this chapter.

While dance studies texts from the mid-twentieth-century have excluded groups such as African-Americans and Native-Americans, dance scholars have not excluded gay and lesbian choreographers and performers, but have closeted their gayness.[2] Hence, Limón does not need to be written into dance studies, but his stagings of non-normative gender and sexuality do. Limón did not address queerness explicitly in his choreography, but his dances presented homosocial spaces and a queer sensibility that re-shaped notions of heteronormativity at the foundation of mid-century American modern dance. Focusing on Limón's all-male dance, *The Traitor* (1954), which refers to Judas Iscariot's betrayal of Jesus Christ, this chapter examines how Limón used biblical narratives to a reconfigure prewar conventions for staging male bodies. As I will show, biblical narratives provided Limón with a textual framework through which he generated the strategic approaches necessary to meet an increasingly conservative postwar political arena energized by the Red Scare.

The Traitor was one of a series of dances based on biblical themes that Limón choreographed in the 1950s. Biblical narratives gave Limón and his work a moral legitimacy and gravity that could offset perceptions of him as both queer and non-white. By couching his queer brown body within a biblical frame, Limón could "do" his non-normative identities. And by doing so, broaden the possibilities for dancers and audiences to experience a more complicated performance of masculinity. Biblical narratives also allowed him to queer modern dance without abandoning the prewar expressionist lineage from which he came. As Michel de Certeau writes,

> [w]ithout leaving the place where he has no choice but to live and which lays down its law for him, he establishes within it a degree of plurality and creativity. By an art of being in between, he draws unexpected results from his situation.[3]

Because Limón did not proclaim to work for a wider collective of queer or non-normative groups does not limit the dissidence in his works. As I will show, his choreography was part of collaboration with other artists, producers, and organizations that produced social spaces in which non-normative and dissident representations could move to the mainstream.

Biblical dances in proto-modern dance

Limón's status as a leading choreographic figure in the 1950s was made, in large part, by the resounding successes of his biblical story ballets, which along with *The Moor's Pavane* (1949), became his most often performed and widely known dances. In chronological order, Limón's biblical dances include *The Exiles* (1950) based on the expulsion of Adam and Eve from the Garden of Eden; *The Visitation* (1952) based on "the Annunciation," the angel Gabriel's announcement to Mary that she would conceive the Son of God; *The Traitor* (1954) based on the story of Jesus Christ and Judas Iscariot; *There is a Time* (1956) based on passages from the book of Ecclesiastes; *Missa Brevis* (1958), literally a "small mass" in honor of the Polish people's struggles after World War II; and lastly, *The Apostate* (1959), based on Julian the Apostate's struggle between Christianity and Greco-Roman Polytheism. Of these dances, *The Exiles* is occasionally performed by the Limón Company but rarely licensed, the choreography for *The Visitation* and *The Apostate* have not survived in the Limón Company's repertory, *The Traitor* had an auspicious beginning, but is now rarely performed, and *There is a Time*, and *Missa Brevis* are widely recognized as "masterpieces" of mid-twentieth-century American modern dance and are often re-staged.[4]

Of course, Limón was not the first twentieth-century choreographer to embrace biblical narratives. As Giora Manor writes,

> the list of modern choreographers inspired by the Bible is a long one. To name but a few: Martha Graham, Lester Horton, Harald Kreutzberg, Glen Tetley, Charles Weidman, Norman Walker, Anna Sokolow, and Serge Lifar; Aurel von Milloss, and John Neumeier in the classical ballet sphere.[5]

Although these choreographers took varied approaches to biblical texts, they all benefitted from the legitimacy, cultural familiarity, and gravity embedded within the texts, as well as the historical and spiritual framework that obviated unwanted allegation of "excessive" or non-normative sexuality.

The biblical, spiritual, and religious narratives depicted by choreographers in the 1910s and 1920s, cannot be separated from Orientalist frameworks. In the United States, Ruth St. Denis' work was at the forefront of this movement. Beginning with *Radha*, her 1906 dance inspired by a poster of Egyptian Deities cigarettes. St. Denis drew on Orientalist frameworks to develop a choreographic strategy through which she complicated representations of gender and embodiments of sexuality. Although riddled with issues of minstrelsy and appropriation that would later denigrate her standing, St. Denis used spiritual and Orientalist narratives to control the means of her artistic production and complicate the objectification of her body. Rather than the limited perception of women as natural and maternal, the Orientalist framework allowed St. Denis and her colleagues to assert themselves in the public sphere as subjects whose sexual identity was not fully controlled by patriarchal systems. Although St. Denis' work focused primarily on Eastern spiritual traditions, she also choreographed dances based on biblical narratives. These include *Jephthah's Daughter* in 1918 and *Dancer at the Court of King Ahasuerus* in 1919 (the dancer portrayed Esther).

Outside of the United States, Maud Allan was squarely situated at the intersection of Orientalism and biblical narratives with her 1907 *Dance of Salome*. Like St. Denis, Allan combined Orientalist and biblical bodies as a way to gain artistic legitimacy and the respect of critics and audiences. Amy Koritz argues that Allan's *The Vision of Salome* presented the public with a subversive staging of female sexuality and the racial Other in which Allan diminished the distance between East and West as well as the distance between a domestic femininity and a public female sexuality.[6] While Allan's use of the Salome narrative has been widely discussed, there were other choreographers who also drew on the narrative.[7] Loie Fuller performed the role of Salome at the Comedie Parisienne in 1895, four years after Oscar Wilde's play was published in French. Unlike Allan, Fuller's performances were not associated with Wilde and avoided the controversies that enveloped Allan's work. Lester Horton also made ample use of the story, presenting at least six dances based on the Salome narrative. Starting with his 1932 *Salome*, which was presented as his first "choreodrama" and ending with *The Face of Violence* (1950).[8]

More so than any of the choreographers mentioned above, Denishawn Co-Director Ted Shawn integrated biblical narratives and Christian thought into modern dance. This integration was not a new or sudden occurrence for Shawn, whose relationship to the bible developed prior to his dance career. As an adolescent, when studying to become a Methodist minister he contracted diphtheria that left him temporarily paralyzed from the waist down. As a remedy, he enlisted in dance lessons, and never looked back. And although Shawn would draw heavily on Native-American and Orientalist narratives for choreographic material throughout his career, biblical narratives were always an important part of his choreographic output. He began producing biblical ballets in 1915 with *Joseph's Legend* and continued with *Miriam: Sister of Moses* (1919), *23rd Psalm* (1921), *Negro Spirituals* (1930), *Job: a Masque for Dancing* (1931), *Dream of Jacob* (1949), and *Song of Songs* (1951). Like his female counterparts, Shawn used the convergence of religion and dance to normalize his performance of gender and build an American identity for himself and his artform.

The year of 1915 was a big year for Shawn. In addition to joining with St Denis, he began a five-year program of study with the Delsarte instructor Henrietta Hovey. The Delsarte method proved to be a seamless fit with his training as a Methodist minister and dancer. And although St. Denis was also familiar with Delsarte's work, Shawn was primarily responsible for incorporating it into Denishawn's training as well as using it to construct their Orientalist/Christian hybrid approach to embodiment. Through this approach, Shawn and St.

Denis could normalize the dangerous sexuality of Oriental bodies within a Christian framework. This created a space for dancers to display and enjoy their sexuality, but rather than encounter the default reading of sexuality as depraved, they could be read as vessels channeling spiritual qualities and a morally edifying experience.

"He knew it was all wrong"

Prior to his work with St Denis and Hovey, Shawn searched for dance instructors, mentors, and partners but came up empty-handed. In a 1975 lecture, Walter Terry discussed Shawn's pre-Denishawn days when male dancers seeking role models or instructors had no recourse but to look to female impersonators:

> Ted Shawn told me himself … Men, because they couldn't get jobs as dancers, imitated the female. That was the way to get into it. And he said he was most influenced, when he started, by a male dancer, who we would call it in drag today, but in those days it was perfectly proper, there were a great many female impersonators, who did a dance very much like Maud Allan, *Salome* … And he [Shawn] saw this female impersonator do it, he saw him do Spanish dancing as a female in Denver and he said he learned how to dance from watching this man doing female things. And he said he knew it was all wrong.[9]

In addition to learning from female impersonators, Terry also discussed how Shawn used sections of travelogues as a learning tool. Terry comments:

> You'd get about 30 seconds of somebody hopping about in a tribal dance maybe a little bit of a Watusi, or "today we visit storied Seville," and you'd get one zapateado and one finger snap. And so he just grabbed on to all these things and made a technique in 1911 based on this and a few ballet lessons he had in Denver. And that's how it all began. There was no other way. There was no place to study.[10]

It is a fascinating set of ambitions, contradictions, and skills that Shawn developed, balanced, and fashioned into a career. Even though he "knew it was all wrong" to train by watching men who "imitated the female," Shawn's early studies not only reveal the dearth of male dancers, but the cultural and economic regulations and codes that inhibited men from pursuing dance. By merging these non normative gender performances with colonial-based travelogues Shawn was uniquely poised to collaborate with St. Denis and begin the Denishawn experiment. In a way, it seems that the lack of men in dance acted as a vacuum within which his hubris and privilege could fuse with a colonialist rationale entitling him to appropriate the non-Western dance cultures he viewed in travelogues. Shawn's fusion of queer subcultures and non-Western cultures proved to be a powerful influence in modern dance's conventions for staging race and gender.

Limón's wholeness

When Limón arrived in New York City in 1929, the terms used to discuss male gender and sexuality operated within a different set of values and meanings than those currently held.[11] As George Chauncey writes,

> the hetero-homosexual binaries, the sexual regime now hege-
> monic in American culture, is a stunningly recent creation ...
> Only in the 1930s, 1940s and 1950s did the now-conventional
> division of men into "homosexuals" and "heterosexuals," based
> on the sex of their sexual partners, replace the division of men
> into "fairies" and "normal men."[12]

Chauncey argues that a heightened anxiety about homosexuality developed in the 1930s that resulted in more intense police actions and governmental regulations against men perceived as "gay." This, in turn, prompted a shift from a prewar "gay world" to a mid-century subculture of "the closet."[13]

It was within this context that Limón joined the Humphrey/ Weidman Dance Company, a membership he held for ten years. During that decade, it was an open secret in the dance world that Limón and Charles Weidman were romantic partners. Their break up in 1940 was a primary reason for Limón leaving the company. Humphrey/Weidman Dance Company alumna, Nona Schurman comments:

> He [Limón] and Charles [Weidman] had been together, of
> course, for years at the Tenth St. ménage as we used to call it,

the Tenth St apartment, and so apparently Charles apparently got infatuated with ... [Peter Hamilton] ... José says it's either Pete or me. So, Charles made up his mind and said its Pete.[14]

Limón left the company and moved to the San Francisco area for two years, choreographing and producing concerts with May O'Donnell, from the Graham Company, and her husband, the musical composer, Ray Green.

In an interview with Marion Horosko, dancer Peter Hamilton recounts his introduction to the Humphrey/Weidman Company:

> They all lived on 10th Street at that point. A large household. Charles and Doris and Pauline Lawrence, and José, and Betty Joiner our costume designer, and Perkins Harnley another designer, they all lived in a very large apartment ... Doris had just married Leo. And that kind of fascinated me too, as an outsider. A kind of design for living ... I felt that they all lived separate lives in separate cocoons in separate rooms and they only had one meeting time, like in the evening. Where they would discuss a ballet, or dinner, and they would all go their own separate ways. It wasn't the kind of family where they were necessarily intertwined as a family in a living room or that kind of thing. I don't think they even saw each other for breakfast. But their design for living was for their art.[15]

As their work has proven, the ambitions and goals fueling the Humphrey/Weidman group's radical "design for living" would not be contained within a disenfranchised designation as a queer subculture. Their expansion, queering, and discarding of heteronormative roles and familial relationships was not only occurring in their household, but also on the modern dance stage, the venue through which they would ultimately gain recognition in the mainstream performing arts world. Manning touches on this move in her analysis of Humphrey's *Day on Earth* (1947), in which Limón performed with two women and a girl. She writes "if one Mexican-American man could make a family with three Euro-American women, then postwar modern dance could accommodate multiracial casting, domestic containment, and the open secret of the closet all at once."[16] This path from an obscure queer subculture to mainstream America revealed different ways that gender was symbiotically bound to racial identity. The queer and subversive activities of Limón's Euro-American house-mates could be filtered through a white privilege that scrubbed them of their queerness, accepted their racial homogeneity, and positioned their work as innovative and creative art. Conversely, Limón's path to the mainstream revealed the circuitous and obstacle-filled path that non-white bodies would confront in engaging modern dance conventions that categorized dance as innovative art or an "ethnic" folk dance.[17]

Although the term, "the closet" currently carries negative connotations associated with hidden lives, Limón's choreographic labor from within the closet reveal the historically contingency of visibility as resistance. Limón's high profile as a leader in the performing arts complicated the idea of a postwar closet as small and hidden. His queerness did not isolate him; he constantly moved through both dominant and marginal cultures and complicated their borders and categories. When Limón began choreographing, successful and widely circulating work by queer artists were commonly framed as anomalies or isolated incidents.[18] But, as musicologist and Women's Studies scholar, Nadine Hubbs shows, many postwar cultural products recognized as iconically American were made by gay artists, even while their non-normative sexuality was closeted.[19] Through his many innovations and successes, Limón proved to be one of many queer artists making work that exemplified the expansion of queer authorship from the cultural margins to the mainstream.

Limón's closeted movement from the margins to the mainstream was contextualized within the emergence of conservative political agendas. As a major force shaping regulations of what constituted normative sexuality, The House Un-American Activities Committee (HUAC), tied its primary concern of the "red threat" of Communism, to the "invisible threat" of homosexuality and began targeting homosexuals in conjunction with Communists. Aligning homosexuality with Communism gave the attacks on homosexuality a conspiratorial rhetoric; under siege by an invisible threat, heterosexual men had to defend their way of life from homosexual men infiltrating their normal world.[20, 21]

HUAC's investigation of the arts as a central avenue through which queer artists were "invading" heterosexual America, was in a way, restricted by their role as a government agency. They were compelled to recognize the Eisenhower Administration's effort to integrate artists into the US Cold War efforts. The President's Emergency Fund for International Affairs was an important part of this effort. This Fund engaged artists as emissaries, sending them and their work throughout the world as examples of artistic freedom, capitalism, and democracy. The José Limón Dance Company was the first dance company chosen for this program, thrusting Limón into a new and higher level of visibility. As a non-white cultural ambassador for the United States' State Department, Limón was a valuable example of diversity and racial tolerance in the US. This new alignment with the State Department made Limón less vulnerable to homophobic critiques. In other words, critics who were targeting gay men in the arts, such as Limón, were forced to revise their strategies to account for Limón's alignment with the state.

While the Otherness of Limón's brown skin and Mexican heritage was an asset to the State Department and could be assimilated into Limón's role as a US cultural ambassador, his queerness could not. Given the pathologized categorization of homosexuality at mid-century, queerness would overpower other characteristics of Limón's identity and impede his ability to represent the United States.[22] This situation exemplifies Limón's fragmented persona. As a queer brown man, Limón's identity as an American artist relied on the absenting of some aspects of his identity while others remained present. His race, ethnicity, and ancestry could be explicitly presented, but his queerness could only be implied. Although these complex aspects could not be merged into a unified self, Limon could present a unified and whole dance. Limón was a master at integrating multiple compositional elements into a seemingly inevitable and unified whole. The complexity of his groupings, deftness of execution, and linearity of narrative came together in a way that made the choreography seem inevitable. The unification of the compositional elements could be seen as pointing to a preordained collectivity. This "choreographed wholeness" countered Limón's fragmented body as well as the fragmented and disrupted postwar society. And when situated within biblical narratives, it represented the whole body of the choreographer through which audiences could imagine a deeper and more significant body-spirit connection. Limón's "choreographed wholeness" was a welcome communal experience, a spiritual gathering that was becoming more difficult to access in contemporary times.

Institutions

In 1954, the American Dance Festival awarded its first "commission for choreography" to Limón, who used it to create *The Traitor*. This was one of many awards and honors that Limón received from multiple institutions over the course of his career. It exemplifies the mutually constitutive growth between Limón's career and the institutionalization of modern dance. As mentioned in the introduction, my periodization of American modern dance extends from 1930 to 1980. And in many ways Limón's career, which ran from 1929 to 1972, parallels this periodization. From his early years at the Bennington Dance Festival as a dancer, to his predominate presence at the American Dance Festival as an established choreographer, and through to his foundational role in the dance division at The Juilliard School of Music, Limón played a central role in the development of modern dance's primary institutions.[23]

Limón's association with The Bennington Dance Festival began as a member of the Humphrey/Weidman Dance Company, a company that was in residence at Bennington from its opening in 1934 until 1939.[24] In 1937 Limón was selected, with Anna Sokolow and Esther Junger, as the first Bennington Fellows, and was awarded resources to create original choreography, which he used to choreograph *Danza de la Muerte (Dance of Death)*. And in the 1939 Bennington Festival, Limón premiered his five-part solo, *Danzas Mexicanas*, which would later serve as seed choreography for his dance, *La Malinche* (1949).

In 1948 the Bennington Festival was transformed into the American Dance Festival and from that opening year until 1973, a year after Limón's death, the José Limón Dance Company acted as the American Dance Festival's resident company. Along with Humphrey, Limón was a perennial member of the American Dance Festival teaching staff; Humphrey from 1948 to the year of her death in 1958 and Limón from 1948 to 1968. (As if to toll the bell of things to come, Humphrey's absence from the teaching staff in 1959 coincided with Merce Cunningham's presence on the staff.)[25] Additionally, the José Limón Dance Company offered dances for repertory classes every year from 1948 to 1964, after which they offered pieces intermittently. And except for the 1960 season, the Limón Company premiered dances every year from the Festival's 1948 opening until 1967. Finally, when the American Dance Festival created an advisory board in 1959, Limón and Pauline Lawrence Limón were selected as board members. Pauline Lawrence Limón served on the board until 1968 and Limón until the board dissolved in 1970.

The Traitor

Not only was *The Traitor* Limón's first all-male dance, it was the first all-male dance by a major choreographer since 1940, when Shawn disbanded Ted Shawn and His Men Dancers.[26] And it would not be until Matthew Bourne's *Swan Lake* in 1995 that another major all-male cast would be presented. Michael Hollander, an original cast member, recalls Limón talking about *The Traitor* as part of his aspiration to show "what a group of men could signify."[27] Hollander suggests that *The Traitor* was Limón's attempt to create a male alternative to the powerful homosocial worlds of Graham's all-female ballets.

Choreographed to Gunther Schuller's *Symphony for Brass and Percussion* (1950), *The Traitor's* original 1954 cast featured Limón as "The Traitor," Lucas Hoving as "The Leader," and six company members as "His Followers." When *The Traitor* premiered, it was a resounding success. Louis Horst wrote that *The Traitor* was, "a great and beautiful work; undoubtedly, with the possible exception of the *Moor's Pavane*, the finest and most powerful work Mr. Limón has ever created."[28] Walter Terry, dance critic for the New York Herald Tribune, called it, "a contemporary dance drama of expressive beauty and enormous emotional power."[29]

Formally, I find Limón's choreography in *The Traitor* to be among his most sophisticated.[30] His group sections deftly coordinate many voices happening simultaneously. Duets share the stage with quartets that weave together to transform into trios or solos all while fluidly moving on and off the stage. As in all of Limón's story ballets, he uses these abstract elements and arrangements as the foundation on which to construct the characters and plot. Even though *The Traitor* was a story ballet, Limón's goal was to tell the story as much as possible through abstraction rather than mimeticism; choreographic structure rather than costume; form rather than gesture. *The Traitor* is at its strongest when Limón is successful in using these formal structures of the dance to share the story-telling task, and at its weakest when Limón relies too heavily on mimetic gestures.

Limón's mimetic gestures of fighting and violence helped to frame the dancers within a normative masculinity, even while dancers were partnering and touching each other in non-normative ways. Limón augmented this mimeticism with abstract movement, which connected Limón's choreography to mid-century assumptions of abstract art as "advanced" and modernist. When this fusion of mimeticism and abstraction was contextualized within the familiarity

of biblical narratives, audience could construct an artistically sophisticated and heteronormative viewing position. It allowed audiences to
read Limón's dances as an abstracted spiritually based high art, while
simultaneously using biblical texts to obfuscate the intimate physical
bonding occurring in the all-male cast.

Dance critic Anna Kisselgoff argued that *The Traitor* was a particularly pictorial dance, in which Limón created distinct visual tableaus
as a way to move the plot along.[31] And as part of this pictorial
approach, lighting design played a pronounced role, more so than
most of Limón's other dances. There is a heavy use of mottled lighting that creates a kind of chiaroscuro effect in which the dancers are
alternately in shadow or light. While chiaroscuro in painting is most
often used to unify pictures, in *The Traitor*, it seems to amplify dis-
tances and confuse spatial arrangements.

This mottled lighting design is contrasted by a single, white,
downstage center, pool of light for Limón's solo. It is a nightmarish
solo reminiscent of his role as a tormented dreamer grappling with
malicious specters in Humphrey's *Nightspell* (1951).[32] Throughout
this solo Limón's focus is inward and downward. From his prostrate
position at the beginning of the solo, he gradually makes his way to
standing, mimes the act of pulling a bag of coin from his shirt, and
reluctantly counts the cost of his betrayal. The single lighting cue for
Limón's solo is the highest contrast cue in the dance. Paradoxically,
rather than bringing Limón into a lighted place, it accentuates the
depth and power of blackness that surrounds him leaving Limón
small, isolated, and overwhelmed. The stark contrast in lighting
offers a Manichean presentation of good and evil that re-tells a melo-
dramatic morality tale in which systemic forces are diminished and
the charismatic performances of individual dancers are emphasized.

Given the Red Scare's oppressive conservative climate within
which Limón was worked, ideas of surveillance abound in *The
Traitor*. The dance opens on an empty stage that is encircled by a set
representing an arched colonnade. Slowly, dancers emerge from
behind the colonnade into the performing space. Limón writes that
the dancer's movement phrases:

> were based on those of persons who enter looking back to see
> whether they had been detected or followed. Their walks and
> body attitudes were those of uncertainty and furtiveness. Once
> safely in this gathering place they would scrutinize each other's
> faces to see that they were the right ones.[33]

To show this, the dancers enter the space intermittently, in solos, duets, and trios. Scanning behind and about them as they enter, the dancers move erratically as they survey and are surveyed. The layered message is clear: while audiences can read this movement as the story of Christ's apostles striving to move undetected by Roman guards, it can also be read as the policing of marginalized and queered groups in Limón's contemporary times.

Hollander describes moments in *The Traitor's* choreographic process:

> in the middle of these May days and June days before we got off to Connecticut College, there would occur these moments when this rehearsal would break down before you knew it, into gay camping ... the younger newer dancers couldn't participate, it alienated, it was difficult ... But here was a dance all about this male ideal that he [Limón] was now trying to re-introduce into the conversation of dance as a possibility. And it was hard, especially as a later adolescent in there ... what I'm describing is vivid only because it was so rare. That it was just a moment when something parts and it would close back up.[34]

Hollander's anxieties open questions about the operation of queerness in categories of high and low art, within which modern dance functioned, as well as in the activities engaged by leadership figures. How did queerness operate and move between the categories inhabited by Limón's idealized homosocial dance and "gay camping?" And how did gay camping align with Limón's position as company director, choreographer, and leader within the genre of modern dance? And finally, how did it fit within the compulsory heterosexuality that contextualized Limón and his work? For example, when asked if Limón's sexuality was ever talked about, Limón Company alumnus Peter Sparling replied,

> never. I only knew that he lived with Pauline at the farm in New Jersey ... that he lived up on 72d Street when he was in New York ... I knew that he had gay men in his company, that it was very much a part of the scene, but his role in relationship to all that, I just assumed that he was a straight man.[35]

Textual beginnings

Given the widespread acclaim that Limón's biblical dances received, it is clear that critics and audiences viewed them as vital and relevant stories that needed to be told, rather than as reductive reproductions of a past time. The desire for biblical stories was not limited to modern dance. There was a kind of fervor for these texts in the postwar cultural imaginary. At the time of its premiere, *The Traitor* paralleled a nationwide growth in religious interest, putting Limón's work in dialogue with national conversations on religion. Historian George Nash writes,

> [I]n 1940 fewer than 50 percent of the American people were church members; by 1955, 60 percent had joined. These years also witnessed the spectacular rise of Billy Graham, the addition of "under God" to the "Pledge of Allegiance," and the printing of "In God we Trust" on certain postage stamps.[36]

Hollywood also recognized and aligned itself with this growth. The biblical epics of Hollywood reached their greatest popularity in the 1950s. From 1946 to 1959, the top grossing films were regularly based on biblical narratives, such as *The Robe* (1953), *The Ten Commandments* (1956), and *Ben Hur* (1959).

The need to tell and experience these biblical stories came in no small part from the need to assuage anxieties and trauma after World War II. Since Limón's biblical story ballets were also historical narratives, audiences could situate *The Traitor* as an ancient world inhabited by characters with whom they could identify and in so doing, escape the anxieties of the postwar world. When Limón transformed into Judas Iscariot he bound the life of the ancients to his own, making the lives and struggles of Iscariot his own, as well as the audience's life and struggles. His embodiment of a biblical figure pointed to the idea that we all carry timeless and universal humanistic traits, that there are truths to being human that always were and always will be.

By identifying with historical figures in this way, audiences and critics could use Limón's embodiment of timeless truths to imagine a time that preceded the complex modern categories of gender and sexuality. As Alan Sinfield proposes, "Shakespeare can't have been gay; not because the bard could not have been so disreputable, but because in his time they didn't have the concept."[37] Similarly, the biblical characters Limón portrayed couldn't have been gay either, which contextualized Limón's all-male cast within a compulsory heterosexuality, allowing audiences to assume that Limón and his dancers were straight.[38] In this way, *The Traitor* could represent a past in which connections between people and a "natural" heteronormative world order was still possible.

Although Humphrey produced dances based on literary sources, such as her 1946 *Lament for Ignacio Sanchez Mejías*, which was based on Federico Lorca's poem of the same name, these literary-based dances were few and far between. More so than Graham, Limón, or Hawkins, Humphrey elided narrative-based dances throughout her career, especially ones with religious associations. After the success of her dance, *The Shakers* (1931), Humphrey commented,

> one thing I vow I will not do again: imitate in art form the rituals of the faithful. No more *Shakers*. I am ashamed of the poverty of my age that it sent me sniffing around people and things that are none of my business.[39, 40]

During the 1930s, Limón followed Humphrey's lead in this matter. From his first choreographic outings in the early 1930s until his split with Humphrey/Weidman in 1940, Limón choreographed musically based, abstract dances that were, with few exceptions, void of literary narrative. The majority of his dances from this period are titled after the music to which he choreographed, such as *Etude in D-flat Major* (1930), his first choreographic outing set to Alexander Scriabin's etude. When not using the title of the musical score, Limón often used names of musical forms, such as *Mazurka* (1931), or *Hymn* (1936). He also used self-referential titles, such as, *Dance* (1933), or *Opus for Three and Props* (1937).

After leaving Humphrey/Weidman in 1940, Limón worked collaboratively with former Graham dancer, May O'Donnell. During this two-year partnership, Limón began experimenting with literary narratives and American themes. The titles of his dances reveal his change to text-based works: *War Lyrics* (1940), *Curtain Raiser* (1941), *The Story is Legend* (1941), and *Three Inventories on Casey Jones* (1941). While these story ballets were the bulk of Limón's output during these two years, he also choreographed two musically based pieces, titling them after their scores; *Alley Tune* (1942) and *Turkey in the Straw* (1942). Limón called these two dances, "elaborations and variation on … authentic forms," which revealed a shift in his musical sources from canonized European composers to "authentic forms" of American music (Limón, *Memoirs* 136).

Although Limón's story ballets of the early 1940s pointed to new forms of experimentation, his foundational change away from musical abstraction and toward narrative-base work came with his, *The Moor's Pavane* (1949), a quartet based on Shakespeare's *Othello*. *The Moor's Pavane* was an immediate success and solidified Limón's place as a leading voice in modern dance. John Martin writes, "Limón has until recently been a satisfactory but not especially distinguished choreographer ... with this latest work [*The Moor's Pavane*] he has definitely made a place for himself among the best of them."[41] This move toward narrative dominated Limón's approach throughout the 1950s and provided the strategic foundation for his radical representations of race and gender discussed below. Through his narrative-based work, Limón joined other mid-twentieth-century choreographers, such as Martha Graham in modern dance, Antony Tudor in ballet, and Agnes De Mille on Broadway to raise choreographic storytelling to new levels of sophistication.

Biblical texts

Many religions use the bible as their foundational text, take its writings literally, and accept it as the original voice of God. However, there are those who not only dispute the literal meaning of the bible, but what parts of the bible belong and which do not. Hence, the bible is both a stable originary text and an unstable collection of books, depending on which community you talk to.[42] This allows a wide range of interpretive models and multiple analyses that can serve a wide range of agendas. Limón's agenda was not to promote a particular religious exegesis of biblical texts, but to address the confluence of modernism, abstraction, and universal humanism. The need to address specific meanings of a particular biblical narrative was tangential to the opportunity it provided to discover and enunciate his place in the world, however complex and unresolved that might turn out to be.

Like all of Limón's biblical story ballets of the 1950s, *The Traitor* reshaped and re-told biblical narratives to address new and shifting social and cultural frameworks. Limón writes that the idea for *The Traitor*:

> as a dramatic dance developed slowly. There was to be a traitor, and a man whom he was to betray, and this man was to have other and devoted followers and there was to be a banquet, and

the moment of betrayal, and the apprehension of the leader and the torment of the false friend and some sort of resolution. As you can see, this was following rather closely the accounts in the New Testament. But it was my intent to use all this only as it pertained to our own time.[43]

Susan Manning and others have discussed how Limón used *The Traitor* to reference events surrounding The House Un-American Activities Committee.[44] Additionally, in the 1960s, after the Red Scare had mostly dissipated, Limón also described *The Traitor* as a response to the execution of Julius and Ethel Rosenberg, writing, "*The Traitor* was the result of my horror at the execution of two Americans, husband and wife, in peacetime, for treason and espionage against their country,"[45,][46] Using a single dance to express different ideas at different times was not an unusual move for Limón and offers another example of his pliable relationship with biblical texts.

Limón was raised Catholic but abandoned the church during high school. He writes:

> the idea of God revolted me ... the expensively elegant congrega-
> tion and the unctuous platitudes of the sermon I found repellent, a
> vicious parody of the Christian spirit, especially since only a few
> blocks away there was hunger, misery, and neglect. I was thinking
> of some pretext to escape this odious place when the organ began
>   This was the opening of the Passion of St. Matthew ... I wept
> with rapture and anguish, with the unendurable pain that only
> beauty inflicts ... I will be forever grateful for this first encounter
> with that voice of God, Johann Sebastian Bach.[47]

Limón's relationship to "repellent" religious dogma but deep rever-
ence for music reveals his complicated relationship with religion and
theatre. His biblical story ballets operated in a space that alternately
merged and separated religion and theatre. On the one hand, his
dance training and choreography were sacred practices through
which dancers could connect to profound states of being. On the
other, he adapted the text to engage the secular world and respond
to politically charged ideas. Certainly, Limón's interpretation of the
Holy Book, with his messages of tolerance and acceptance of non-
normative sexualities ran counter to many conservative religious
communities who held acts of homosexuality a sin against God's
natural order.

An ancillary modernism

When Limón choreographed *The Traitor*, the postwar terrain of concert dance was shifting. Ballet was being recognized as modernist, modern dance and ballet were being welcomed onto Broadway, and a new generation of avant-gardists, led by the work of Merce Cunningham and John Cage, was gaining ground. The relevance of the expressionistic traditions and practices personified by Limón and Graham were being questioned, especially when these traditions were based on narrative. As Gay Morris argues, Limón's story ballets were no longer holding the value they once did as beacons of modernism, instead they were becoming "the trouble with modern dance."[48]

Much of the criticism aimed at Limón's work referenced the art criticism of Clement Greenberg. Greenberg's arguments for medium specificity and self-referentiality played a significant role in establishing divisions between the expressionistic works of Graham and Limón and the vanguard experimentations of Cunningham and the Judson School. Greenberg writes, "painting, sculpture, music, poetry become more concrete by confining themselves strictly to that which is most palpable to them, namely their mediums, and by refraining from treating or imitating what lies outside the province of their exclusive effects."[49] In this Greenbergian context, text and music become elements external to dance, making Limón's story ballets something outside of, behind, or less than modernist.

However, the Greenbergian position also divorces the medium of dance, the human body, from the ways it bears and performs social markings of gender, nation, race, and sexuality. It's "disinterested" analysis of the dancing body usurped credibility from Limón's use of narrative as a way to navigate these social markings. Because Limón relied on stories in ways that his white counterparts did not need to, his particular agendas and interests in using narrative come to the surface when they are examined as social interactions rather than as isolated aesthetic elements. In the way that Cunningham disrupted the importance of a central and singular point in space by making all points of the stage important, so Limón disrupted the importance of a central and singular Euro-American identity by making non-white identities important. Hence, in order to explore the social functions of Limón's storytelling, his narrative-based work must be pulled out of the Greenbergian framework and examined how it functioned in an ancillary modernism. A modernism through which he, as a queer brown man, could realize his ambitions in ways he could not in a postwar scene that had left conventions for staging race and gender largely intact.

Who needs metaphors?

In addition to narrative, Limón used metaphors to frame the staging of his queer brown body. As Louis O. Mink argues, storytelling and metaphor are two of the central cognitive processes used to create meaning and make sense of one's place in the world. He writes,

> even though narrative form may be for most people associated with fairy tales, myths, and the entertainments of the novel, it remains true that narrative is a primary cognitive instrument— an instrument rivaled, in fact, only by theory and by metaphor as irreducible ways of making the flux of experience comprehensible.[50]

One of Limón's regularly used metaphors was what he called "voices of the body," a metaphor of the body as an orchestra in which different body parts were different instruments.[51] For example, the elbow could be a viola while the hips simultaneously acted as a xylophone. Imagining the body as an orchestra provided choreographers, performers, instructors, and students a way to choreograph, improvise, and perform by assembling parts of the body in never-ending combinations and variations. Limón's voices of the body transformed dancing bodies into orchestral bodies that were able to produce a kind of visual music. As an instrument to be played, Limón's musical body expressed and illustrated the score he danced to.

Dance scholar Mark Franko uses the terms "classical expression theory" to analyze such musical-expressionistic approaches.[52] Franko theorizes music as the initial impression of the "soul" of the dancer, who then translates this impression into physical movement. He writes, "for the dancer it could be charted: Music > Feeling > Dance."[53] This charting is seen in Limón's description of his choreographic process for his dance, *Chaconne* (1942), which was mentioned at the beginning of this chapter. Limón recalls the process:

> locked up in this room, with these sounds [Bach's chaconne] penetrating my sensibilities and my bones and tissues, the music took full command. At times I would abandon myself to a kind

of trance, stand totally motionless, and say inaudibly: "Tell me,
tell me what to do here, and here, and there." Then, the will
and the intelligence would take over, and what the intuition had
gathered from the music was carefully and rigorously formalized
to comply with the thematic premise. The dance emerged,
formal, majestic, elegant, and above all beautiful.[54]

As in Franko's classical expression theory, Limón's process began
with Bach's music, followed by an abandonment of his self, then a
"letting go" of his mind to "feel" the music. Finally, his feelings are
"carefully and rigorously" formed into a choreographed dance.
Socially, the implications embedded in the hierarchical relationship
between intuition, intelligence, rigor, and form were of particular
importance to Limón's status as a modernist artist. More so than his
Euro-American colleagues, it was necessary for Limón to subsume an
intuitive, embodied experience to intellect and formal rigor. For as a
culturally marked body, intuition without will and intelligence
offered another way to locate Limón's choreography and performances as "natural" and "gifted" rather than "skilled" and "trained."
    As Euro-American dancers, Hawkins and Cunningham did not
need the mediation of a metaphorical body. Since Hawkins and
Cunningham's avant-garde fusion of body and self operated within
modern dance's racial representational conventions they could simply
move without the need to be anything but what they were. As Susan
Foster writes of Cunningham, "his conception of the dancing body
fuses body and self by immersing the self in the practical pursuit of
enhancing the body's articulacy."[55]
    Peggy Phelan offers a way to explore this issue through
metonymy, writing:

> In moving from the grammar of words to the grammar of the
> body, one moves from the realm of metaphor to the realm of
> metonymy ... In performance, the body is metonymic of self, of
> character, of voice, of "presence." But in the plentitude of its
> apparent visibility and availability, the performer actually dis-
> appears and represents something else—dance, movement, and
> sound character, art.[56]

Although Hawkins and Cunningham could move from the
"grammar of words to the grammar of the body" and "become"
dance or movement, Limón could not. When Limón portrayed a

literary character, for example Judas Iscariot in *The Traitor*, the character could be superimposed onto Limón and Limón's brown body could "disappear" into the character. However, without a character or story, Limón's culturally marked body would not "disappear" into a metonymical relationship with movement. Rather, it would become available to essentializing or racialized readings.

Gazing queerly

The heteronormative gaze was the dominant mode of viewing for American modern dance audiences throughout Limón's career. Ideological frameworks to view and discuss dancing bodies outside of this gaze, such as feminist and queer theory, were only just being recognized on a wider scale. As Manning has shown, audience members do not share a common point of view, only a time and place of viewing.[57] Each individual constructs their readings from their particular relationship to a broad set of social power systems. A particular position does not mandate a particular point of view. Manning theorizes a model of spectatorship she refers to as "cross-viewing," in which audience members from different classes and cultures have opportunities to view representations of race, gender, and sexuality, in different ways and from different perspectives.[58] Rather than a singular mode of viewing, Manning reveals how multiple points of view were possible, allowing for Limón's choreography and performances to be read in multiple ways, queered as well as straight.

Furthermore, an audience member's interpretation of a performance also involves their previous knowledge of choreographic codes and conventions, as well as their skill in critically assessing them. For example, how did different audience members understand markers of queerness, straightness, or gayness in Limón's choreography, and what were these markers? The way the dancers moved? The stylization of the movement? The choice of costuming? The presence of traits in the dance that were culturally marked as gay or masculine? All-male casts or same-sex partnering? The open secret that Limón and other male dancers were gay or bisexual? The assumption that male dancers were gay or were rumored to associate with gay colleagues?

Limón's choreography and performances are not queer, straight, or gay except in individual audience readings. There is no inherent queer or straight link between dances, choreographers, spectators, and dancers. One does not need to identify as queer to read queerly and in turn, because someone identifies as gay or queer does not necessarily mean that they would read Limón's dances gayly or queerly. Limón's marginality as a male dancer and queer man may have offered particular insights that challenged him and heightened his awareness, but his marginality and queerness were not inherent or essential reasons for his creativity. The notion that Limón's marginality or queerness could account for his creativity downplays the importance of his contributions to the genre of modern dance by diminishing Limón's rational, problem solving processes he used in his choreography, as well as his disciplined approach to his training and performances.

Conclusion

Limón's biblical story ballets were at the center of his postwar choreographic project, a project that was pivotal in realizing many of modern dance's prewar goals to broaden its audience base and legitimize its standing. And although Limón's non-normativity was closeted within these biblical story ballets, there was a performance of queerness available for those looking, and whether it was seen or unseen, it played a central role in moving the genre of modern dance from a marginalized subculture into the mainstream. As Jeff Weinstein writes, "[t]here is no such thing as a gay sensibility and it has an enormous impact on the culture."[59] The role that *The Traitor* played in making modern dance a space in which non-normative activities between and about male homosociality could occur provided a model for future choreographers seeking to stage a more nuanced masculinity. In this way, Limón acted as a harbinger of new representational strategies in which queer and culturally marked bodies could create identity and understand their place in the world.

Notes

1 Limón, José and Lynn Garafola. *José Limón: An Unfinished Memoir.* Hanover, NH: University Press of New England, 1998.
2 Desmond, Jane. "Embodying Difference: Issues in Dance and Cultural Studies." *Meaning in Motion: New Cultural Studies of Dance*, edited by Jane Desmond. Durham: Duke University Press, 1997.
3 de Certeau, Michel, Luce Giard, and Pierre Mayol. *The Practice of Everyday Life.* Minneapolis: University of Minnesota Press, 1998.
4 Dances in Limón's oeuvre referring to biblical texts outside of the 1950s include: *Eden Tree* (1945), *Song of Songs* (1947), and *Psalm* (1967).
5 Manor, Giora. "The Bible as Dance." *Dance Magazine.* 1978: 56–85.

6 Koritz, Amy. "Dancing the Orient for England: Maud Allan's 'The Vision of Salome'." *Theatre Journal*. Vol. 46, No. 1. March 1994: 63–78. 69–70.
7 Ruth St. Denis performed her dance based on the story of Salome as late as 1948.
8 Horton used the term choreodrama to describe his style of dance-theatre.
9 Terry, Walter. "The Male Dancer." Harvard Summer Dance Center. July 31, 1975.
10 Terry, Walter. "The Male Dancer." Harvard Summer Dance Center. July 31, 1975.
11 Sources differ on Limón's date of arrival in New York; some have it in late 1928, others in early 1929.
12 Chauncey, George. *Gay New York: Gender, Urban Culture, and the Makings of the Gay Male World, 1890–1940*. New York: Basic Books, 1994.
13 Chauncey, George. *Gay New York: Gender, Urban Culture, and the Makings of the Gay Male World, 1890–1940*. New York: Basic Books, 1994.
14 Schurman, Nona. Interview by Ann Vachon.
15 Hamilton, Peter. Interview by Marion Horosko. June 19, 1967.
16 Manning, Susan. *Modern Dance, Negro Dance: Race in Motion*. Minneapolis: University of Minnesota Press, 2004.
17 Laclau, Ernesto. *Emancipation(s)*. Verso, 2007.
18 Sherry, Michael. *Gay Artists in Modern American Culture: An Imagined Conspiracy*. Chapel Hill: University of North Carolina Press, 2007.
19 Hubbs, Nadine. *The Queer Composition of Americas Sound: Gay Modernists, American Music, and National Identity*. University of California Press, 2004.
20 Sherry, Michael. *Gay Artists in Modern American Culture· An Imagined Conspiracy*. Chapel Hill: University of North Carolina Press, 2007.
21 These homophobic anxieties were stoked by the 1948 Kinsey Report, *Sexual Behavior in the Human Male*, which suggested that illicit sexual activity by men was far more widespread than anyone had thought. They were also amplified by the 1952 declaration by the American Psychiatric Association that categorized homosexuality as a mental illness.
22 Sherry, Michael. *Gay Artists in Modern American Culture: An Imagined Conspiracy*. Chapel Hill: University of North Carolina Press, 2007.
23 The name was changed from The Juilliard School of Music to The Julliard School in 1969.
24 The Bennington School of the Dance was founded in 1934 at Bennington College in Bennington, Vermont and the Bennington Festival, which produced new dance pieces in coordination with the school, was established in 1935.
25 The American Dance Festival honored Humphrey in 1960 with the creation of The Doris Humphrey Fellowship, which supported emerging choreographers.
26 Limón did choreograph *Diálogos* (1951), a duet for himself and Lucas Hoving. Limón's subsequent all-male dances include, *Scherzo* (1955), *The Emperor Jones* (1956), and *The Unsung* (1970).

27 Hollander, Michael. "Interview with Michael Hollander and James Payton." By Ann Vachon. 1996.

28 Horst quoted in Anderson, Jack. *The American Dance Festival*. Durham: Duke University Press, 1987.

29 Terry, Walter. "Limón's *The Traitor*." *New York Herald Tribune*. 1954.

30 My analysis of *The Traitor* is largely taken from the March 1957 performance on the DVD, *José Limón: Three Modern Dance Classics*.

31 Kisselgoff, Anna. "When Erick Hawkins sets out to Enlighten." *New York Times*. December 18, 1988.

32 Though commonly referred to as *Nightspell*, its official title is *Quartet No. 1*, referring to its score, Priaulx Rainier's *Quartet for Strings*.

33 Limón, José. "Composing a Dance." *The Juilliard Review*. Vol. 2, No. 1. Winter 1955: 17–23.

34 Hollander, Michael. "Interview with Michael Hollander and James Payton." By Ann Vachon. 1996.

35 Sparling, Peter. Personal interview. 2010.

36 Nash, George. *The Conservative Intellectual Movement in America Since 1945*. New York: Basic Books, 1976.

37 Sinfield, Alan. *Cultural Politics—Queer Reading*. Philadelphia: University of Pennsylvania Press, 1994.

38 Rich, Adrienne. "Compulsory Heterosexuality and Lesbian Existence." *Signs*. Vol. 5, No. 4. 1980: 631–660.

39 Siegel, Marcia B. *Days on Earth: The Dance of Doris Humphrey*. New Haven: Yale University Press, 1987.

40 Humphrey choreographed *The Shakers* in 1931. Based on the religious community known as "Shakers."

41 Martin, John. "The Moor's Pavane." *New York Times*. August 1949.

42 Bial, Henry. *Playing God: The Bible on the Broadway Stage*. University of Michigan Press, 2015.

43 "Composing a Dance." *The Juilliard Review*. Vol. 2, No. 1. Winter 1955: 17–23.

44 Manning, Susan. *Modern Dance, Negro Dance: Race in Motion*. Minneapolis: University of Minnesota Press, 2004.

45 Limón, José. "An American Accent." In *The Modern Dance: Seven Statements of Belief*, edited by Selma Jeanne Cohen. Middletown, CT: Wesleyan University Press. 1966: 17–27.

46 Limón, José. "An American Accent." In *The Modern Dance: Seven Statements of Belief*, edited by Selma Jeanne Cohen. Middletown, CT: Wesleyan University Press. 1966: 17–27.

47 Limón, José, and Lynn Garafola. *José Limón: An Unfinished Memoir*. Hanover, NH: University Press of New England, 1998.

48 Morris, Gay. *A Game for Dancers: Performing Modernism in the Postwar Years, 1945–1960*. Middletown, CT: Wesleyan University Press, 2006.

49 Greenberg, Clement. *The Collected Essays and Criticism*, edited by John O'Brian. Chicago: University of Chicago Press, 1986.

50 Mink, Louis. "Narrative Form as a Cognitive Instrument." In *The History and Narrative Reader*, edited by Geoffrey Roberts. London: Routledge, 2001.

51 "Dancers are Musicians are Dancers." In *José Limón: The Artist Reviewed*, edited by June Dunbar. New York: Routledge. 2002: 9–18.
52 Franko, Mark. *Dancing Modernism/Performing Politics*. Bloomington: Indiana University Press, 1995.
53 Franko, Mark. *Dancing Modernism/Performing Politics*. Bloomington: Indiana University Press, 1995.
54 Limón, José, and Lynn Garafola. *José Limón: An Unfinished Memoir*. Hanover, NH: University Press of New England, 1998.
55 Foster, Susan Leigh. "Dancing Bodies." In *Meaning in Motion: New Cultural Studies of Dance*, edited by Jane Desmond. Durham: Duke University Press, 1997.
56 Phelan, Peggy. *Unmarked: The Politics of Performance*. London; New York: Routledge, 1993.
57 Manning, Susan. *Modern Dance, Negro Dance: Race in Motion*. Minneapolis: University of Minnesota Press, 2004.
58 Manning, Susan. *Modern Dance, Negro Dance: Race in Motion*. Minneapolis: University of Minnesota Press, 2004.
59 Weinstein quoted in *The Celluloid Closet*. Russo, Vito. Harper & Row, 1981.

Works cited

Bial, Henry. *Playing God: The Bible on the Broadway Stage*. Ann Arbor, MI: University of Michigan Press, 2015.

Chauncey, George. *Gay New York: Gender, Urban Culture, and the Makings of the Gay Male World, 1890–1940*. New York: Basic Books, 1994.

de Certeau, Michel, Luce Giard, and Pierre Mayol. *The Practice of Everyday Life*. Minneapolis, MN: University of Minnesota Press, 1998.

Desmond, June. "Embodying Difference: Issues in Dance and Cultural Studies." In *Meaning in Motion: New Cultural Studies of Dance*, edited by Jane Desmond. Durham, NC: Duke University Press, 1997.

Foster, Susan Leigh. "Dancing Bodies." In *Meaning in Motion: New Cultural Studies of Dance*, edited by Jane Desmond. Durham, NC: Duke University Press, 1997.

Franko, Mark. *Dancing Modernism/Performing Politics*. Bloomington, IN: Indiana University Press, 1995.

Greenberg, Clement. *The Collected Essays and Criticism*, edited by John O'Brian. Chicago: University of Chicago Press, 1986.

Hamilton, Peter. Interview by Marion Horosko. June 19, 1967.

Hollander, Michael. "Interview with Michael Hollander and James Payton." By Ann Vachon. 1996.

Horst quoted in Anderson, Jack. *The American Dance Festival*. Durham, NC: Duke University Press, 1987.

Hubbs, Nadine. *The Queer Composition of Americas Sound: Gay Modernists, American Music, and National Identity*. Berkeley, CA: University of California Press, 2004.

Kisselgoff, Anna. "When Erick Hawkins sets out to Enlighten." *New York Times*. December 18, 1988.

Koritz, Amy, "Dancing the Orient for England: Maud Allan's 'The Vision of Salome'." *Theatre Journal*. Vol. 46, No. 1. March 1994: 63–78 69–70.

Laclau, Ernesto. *Emancipation(s)*. London and New York: Verso, 2007.

Limón, José. "An American Accent." In *The Modern Dance: Seven Statements of Belief*, edited by Selma Jeanne Cohen. Middletown, CT: Wesleyan University Press. 1966: 17–27.

Limón, José. "Composing a Dance." *The Juilliard Review*. Vol. 2, No. 1. Winter 1955: 17–23.

Limón, José. "Dancers are Musicians are Dancers." In *José Limón: The Artist Re-viewed*, edited by June Dunbar. New York: Routledge. 2002: 9–18.

Limón, José and Lynn Garafola. *José Limón: An Unfinished Memoir*. Hanover, NH: University Press of New England, 1998.

Manning, Susan. *Modern Dance, Negro Dance: Race in Motion*. Minneapolis, MN: University of Minnesota Press, 2004.

Manor, Giora. "The Bible as Dance." *Dance Magazine*. 1978: 56–85.

Martin, John. "The Moor's Pavane." *New York Times*. August 1949.

Mink, Louis. "Narrative Form as a Cognitive Instrument." In *The History and Narrative Reader*, edited by Geoffrey Roberts. London: Routledge, 2001.

Morris, Gay. *A Game for Dancers: Performing Modernism in the Postwar Years, 1945–1960*. Middletown, CT: Wesleyan University Press, 2006.

Nash, George. *The Conservative Intellectual Movement in America Since 1945*. New York: Basic Books, 1976.

Phelan, Peggy. *Unmarked: The Politics of Performance*. London; New York: Routledge, 1993.

Rich, Adrienne. "Compulsory Heterosexuality and Lesbian Existence." *Signs*. Vol. 5, No. 4. 1980: 631–660.

Russo, Vito. *The Celluloid Closet*. New York: Harper & Row, 1981.

Schurman, Nona. Interview by Ann Vachon.

Sherry, Michael. *Gay Artists in Modern American Culture: An Imagined Conspiracy*. Chapel Hill, NC: University of North Carolina Press, 2007.

Siegel, Marcia B. *Days on Earth: The Dance of Doris Humphrey*. New Haven, CT: Yale University Press, 1987.

Sinfield, Alan. *Cultural Politics—Queer Reading*. Philadelphia, PA: University of Pennsylvania Press, 1994.

Sparling, Peter. Personal Interview. 2010.

Terry, Walter. "The Male Dancer." Harvard Summer Dance Center. July 31, 1975.

Terry, Walter. "Limón's *The Traitor*." *New York Herald Tribune*. 1954.

Figure 3.1 Laura Pettibone Wright as Raccoon in *Plains Daybreak* (1979).

Source: Papadopolous, Peter, "Raccoon, *Plains Daybreak*," 1982, St. Petersburg Times, © Peter Papadopolous/Tampa Bay Times via ZUMA Wire.

Figure 3.2 Erick Hawkins as First Man in *Plains Daybreak* (1979).

Source: Papadopolous, Peter, "Raccoon, *Plains Daybreak*," 1982, St. Petersburg Times, © Peter Papadopolous/Tampa Bay Times via ZUMA Wire.

Figure 3.3 José Limón and company member in *Lament for Ignacio Sanchéz Mejías* (1946).

Figure 3.4 José Limón and company members in *The Emperor Jones* (1956).

Chapter 3

Plains Daybreak

Introduction

The year of 1973 marked the 27th year that the United States and Soviet Union squared off as Cold War antagonists. The issues at hand and their complexities often shifted from year to year, but racial justice and civil rights remained high on propagandistic agendas. The Soviet Union and its allies criticized the United States' record on racial justice and civil rights while the United States countered by claiming superiority through narratives of freedom and democracy. The year of 1973 also marked the Limón Company's first tour to the Soviet Union. In an interview with Billie Mahoney, Leticia Ide, former Limón Company dancer recalled the preparation for the tour in which the "Russian Government Concert Bureau" would only approve the Company's program after viewing the specific dances that the company proposed to present.[1]

One of the dances the Limón Company offered was Limón's *The Emperor Jones* (1958). As discussed in Chapter 5 of this book, *The Emperor Jones* was based on Eugene O'Neill's play of the same name in which Brutus Jones, an African-American pullman porter, becomes emperor of an unnamed Caribbean island. This 1973 production of *The Emperor Jones* featured African-American dancer Clay Taliaferro performing the lead role of Brutus Jones, the role originally danced by Limón. In addition to Taliaferro, the cast included Taliaferro's counterpart, "The White Man," and six male dancers who danced the role of the "native subjects." Taliaferro recalls the audition:

> The Subjects, the other dancers in this work, they were the natives, and you used tan #2 to make the skin dark and they stripped down so the body had to be covered with this make-up

that makes them sort of a brown. Egyptian or tan #2 and they [the Government Concert Bureau] didn't like that idea and I'll never forget as long as I live, that wouldn't work, so we said, what can we do. It wouldn't work choreographically and visually if my Subjects were white so they decided to put them in Indian, American Indian war paint. That they would accept.[2]

The acceptance of "American Indian war paint" by the Russian Government Concert Bureau reveals the disenfranchised and impotent status of Native-Americans in the Cold War's racial politics. It also shows the "surplus symbolic value" of Native-American cultures in that they can be made to stand for something other than themselves, such as Caribbean "native subjects."[3] Conversely, the Bureau's rejection of brown paint as a way to denote Afro-Caribbean identity confirms the inclusion of African cultural identity within Cold War racial politics. The narrative was clear: while Native-American cultural symbols could be used with impunity, there were costs in representing blackness.

This interaction between the genre of modern dance and Native-American cultures was not an anomaly. References and representations of Native-American cultures have been part of modern dance throughout the genre's history. They carry a high representational value for modern dance choreographers, and given Native-Americans' disenfranchised status, have provided choreographers with access to notions of primitivity, "naturalness," and perhaps most importantly, a lineage to an "original" American identity. Philip Deloria examines this malleability of Native-American cultural identities through the idea of "Indianness," which he describes as a set of qualities and attributes, such as primitive and "natural," imposed on Native-Americans by Euro-Americans.[4] Indianness becomes available when Native-American cultures are pulled out of a geopolitical context and emptied of historical and social content. Detached from a specific community, Native-American symbols can then be used to portray a multitude of ideas or bodies, such as *The Emperor Jones'* Caribbean "natives." I keep close to Deloria's notion of Indianness throughout this chapter as I examine how choreographers refer to Native-American cultures as a way to develop their choreography and theories of embodiment.

Dance critic Anna Kisselgoff's review of Erick Hawkins' *Plains Daybreak* (1979) touches on many of the issues this chapter will address. Kisselgoff writes:

Plains Daybreak is one of Mr. Hawkins' ... most subtle transpositions of American Indian culture to the 20th-century theater. The ritual he suggests here is by no means an American Indian ceremony, but the dancers' slightly tilted posture, with knees bent, is certainly derived from Indian dances. The heart of *Plains Daybreak* is a poetic distillation of essences.[5]

Kisselgoff was one of Hawkins' early and career-long champions and as such, her review of *Plains Daybreak* is careful to circumvent issues of minstrelsy and appropriation by positioning Hawkins as a poet-artist transposing and distilling the essence of "American Indian culture." Kisselgoff's rhetorical strategy was not new or limited to the specific production of *Plains Daybreak*. Rather, it exemplifies the parameters of the discourse embedded in the representational practices of early and mid-twentieth-century modern dance choreographers when referring to notions of Native-American cultures.

Periodization

The choreographic convention of drawing on non-Western cultures in order to construct an American identity was a central practice in prewar modern dance. As Susan Manning has shown, this practice began to fade in the early 1940s and diminish more rapidly after World War II, when non-white and indigenous choreographers began to be recognized on their own terms, rather than contextualized within a Euro-American frame.[6] The abandonment of prewar minstrel-based practices left a vacuum that required a new mode of representation, which was eventually filled by a practice Manning calls "mythic abstraction."[7] Mythic abstraction involved eschewing the "'Orientals,' 'primitives,' Native Americans, and African-Americans conjured through the 1930s choreography of Ted Shawn, Martha Graham, and Helen Tamiris" and instead "staged universal subjects without the mediation of bodies marked as culturally other."[8] Manning is quick to address the porousness of periodizing historical practices and notes that the move to mythic abstraction was not completely new, nor did it mark a clear and distinct break from previous practices. She writes that choreographers of the 1930s had already begun using mythic abstraction in the sense that they had already "staged universal subjects without the mediation of bodies marked as culturally other," but after 1940, it became the predominate practice (Manning 2004).

Given this periodization of racial representational strategies, *Plains Daybreak* offers a complex collision of pre and postwar choreographic practices. Hawkins' representational strategy for *Plains Daybreak* has one foot in prewar minstrel-based conventions and one foot in Manning's postwar mythic abstraction. This both and neither position was one Hawkins regularly grappled with. He writes of his positionality as a white American modern dancer in his essay with the all-inclusive title, *Why Does a Man Dance, And What Does He Dance, And Who Should Watch Him?* In it, Hawkins explores the dearth of cultural traditions on which he might build a significant and relevant identity for himself and other Euro-American male dancers. He writes,

> dance for men in America has no prototypic underlying ritual and myth such as the matador in the Spanish bullfight has to give him his challenge, his commitment, his worth and his honor. But unless something equivalent to this is finally created in the soul of the American people a man's dancing will always be inconsequential.[9]

Hawkins' example of the Spanish bullfight is of particular interest for my pairing of Limón and Hawkins. Although Hawkins wrote this article in 1964, it is likely he was referencing Humphrey's 1946 dance, *Lament for Ignacio Sanchez Mejías* in which Limón performed the role of the renowned Spanish bullfighter, Ignacio Sanchez Mejías. *Lament for Ignacio Sanchez Mejías* premiered to great acclaim, became a signature work for Limón, and was in the repertory of the Limón Company for many years. It established Limón as a performer with a level of gravitas and credibility previously unseen in male dancers. As Hawkins writes, the Spanish bullfight, did indeed give Limón "his challenge, his commitment, his worth and his honor" (ibid.). I'll briefly explore how *Lament for Ignacio Sanchez Mejías* became a key work in which Limón catalyzed a shift of representational strategies that previously excluded non-white bodies from performing as universal figures.

Lament for Ignacio Sanchez Mejías

Humphrey's *Lament for Ignacio Sanchez Mejías* debuted at the 1946 Bennington Dance Festival and was immediately hailed a masterwork. It confirmed Humphrey's transformation from a leading prewar choreographer to a postwar one, as well as Limón's position as postwar dance's premier male performer. Norman Lloyd, a long-time colleague and collaborator of Humphrey and Limón's composed the score for *Lament for Ignacio Sanchez Mejías*. He recounts the dance's conception, "Doris [Humphrey] said José [Limón] is in the army, but he is going to be getting out, why don't we give him a dance as a present, and that is what *Lament* became."[10] Costumed in toreador pants, ballet slippers, and a bare-chest, Limón danced a ritualistic bullfight and Sanchez Mejías' death in the ring. He was accompanied by two female Limón Company members reciting lines from Garcia Lorca's poem, one as the Woman of Destiny and the other as the Woman of Compassion.

Although *Lament for Ignacio Sanchez Mejías* was conventional in the sense that it was a narrative-based dance in the expressionist tradition, it becomes a radical gesture through Humphrey's positioning of Limón, a non-white dancer, as a universal figure. Humphrey commented that Limón was meant to "signify the struggle of all men of courage who contend in the ring of Life and who meet a tragic end, to which they are bound by destiny, and to which they must go alone."[11] Concurring with Humphrey, Doris Hering commented, "Humphrey's finest dance for José Limón combines both of her favorite images—the Everyman and the Spaniard. It also presents Limón at his most ennobled."[12] And Margaret Lloyd wrote, "Miss Humphrey lifts the subject into the realm of exalted tragedy, purifying and ennobling the personal theme into a thing of universal implications."[13] Performing the personal as the universal was a well-established convention in modern dance, but before Limón, no non-white dancer was able to do this on such a scale. Through his portrayal of Sanchez Mejías Limón did what neither Euro-American nor African-American dancers had been able to do, perform as both a culturally marked and universal body.

The innovative and subversive nature of this intervention posed problems for many critics and reviewers. They struggled with ways to discuss Humphrey and Limón's non-white universality. For example, Margaret Lloyd proposed, "with his [Limón's] Aztec-Hispanic features, his dark eyes and straight black hair, the virile strength of his broad shoulders, he is virtually typecast in the role of Ignacio Sanchez Mejías."[14] Similarly, Jill Johnston observed, "Humphrey combined her craft at its best with an inspiration from the Garcia Lorca poem and a style especially suited to Limón's great weight and refined Spanish arrogance and Mexican-Indian brutality."[15] Lloyd and Johnston's comments exemplify the difficulty of breaking out of conventional perspectives on race and articulating a new representational strategy as well as the durability of essentialist ideas about race and ethnicity that Limón would encounter throughout his career.

Like Shawn before him, Limón's performance in *Lament for Ignacio Sanchez Mejías* referenced a culturally marked body as a way to attain a masculinity that would counter the feminization of a career in dance. But unlike Shawn, Limón was a culturally marked body and his performance of Sanchez Mejías included his own personal and culturally marked histories that directly related to and impacted his performance. Limón wrote of a childhood memory in his posthumously published memoirs:

> The dance I found so fascinating was the bullfight. No sarabande, chaconne, or passacaglia surpasses the *corrida de toros* in its grave formality, solemnity, sober elegance, grace, and ritual ... Costumed in great splendor and breathtaking colors, the bullfighters evoke an age that knew how to enhance the appearance of a man ... I did not know, as I watched spellbound, that I was watching an art whose gesture and movement would influence me profoundly when I became a dancer. In composing dances, I would look back to this formative experience for guidance and inspiration.[16]

Drawing on his "formative experience" of the bullfight, Limón performed a masculinity that was elegant and graceful without being effeminate, a more nuanced representation of gender than had previously been seen on the modern dance stage. The grave solemnity of the ritual provides a heteronormative framework allowing Limón to take pleasure in the "breathtaking colors" worn by the bullfighters who "evoke an age that knew how to enhance the appearance of a man." It allowed Limón to disassemble his personal histories of nonnormative sexuality and abject Mexican-Indian ancestry and reassemble them into the universal choreographic spectacle that was *Lament*. As Hawkins wrote, it provided Limón with a "ritual or myth" to perform a powerful masculinity, a performative approach that was not available to Hawkins.

Indianness in modern dance—Shawn

In addition to Limon's influential work, Ted Shawn had established a practice of referring to Native-American cultures with which Hawkins' would have to grapple. As Jacqueline Shea Murphy has shown, Shawn played a central role in developing conventions for representing Indianness in modern dance.[17] While on a 1914 dance tour in the Southwest, Shawn had the opportunity to view Native-American dance and wrote that he "discovered a people whose art of dance is so prolific, so inexhaustible in its art content that several life spans could be spent profitably in giving it to the world."[18] Shea Murphy shows how Shawn's Eurocentric view of "discovering" Native-Americans was complicated by his effort to "save" Native-American cultures and dances. Like many of his colleagues, Shawn defended Native-American dance from attacks by the US government and argued that Indian dance was of a high spiritual order and must be preserved. This tension between "discovering" and "saving" Native-American cultures remained a consistent and volatile issue in modern dance's racial representational practices throughout the twentieth century.

Symbols of Native-American cultures played a prominent role in Shawn's concerts throughout his career. For example, he choreographed *Invocation to the Thunderbird* in 1917 and it remained in his repertory until the early 1950s. Shawn's integration of Native-American cultures was driven by the need to remake notions of American masculinity. By performing as an indigenous pre-modern body with ancient connections to "nature," Shawn could exhibit a male body free from the debilitating effects of modern life. This gave him access to ways of moving that were not conventional for men in mainstream America. While Shawn's "Indian dances" may look simple or unsophisticated to our twenty-first-century eyes, they were widely acknowledged as critical successes and a powerful new approach to performing a robust masculinity. In this way, Shawn established a context within which audiences and critics would engage Hawkins' *Plains Daybreak*.

Plains Daybreak

Plains Daybreak premiered at the Adelphi Calderone Theater in Hempstead Long Island in 1979. Alan Hovhaness composed the music, Ralph Dorazio designed the set, Ralph Lee the masks and

costumes, and Robert Engstrom the lighting—all longtime collaborators cherished by Hawkins. The original cast of nine dancers was
comprised of four women and five men. Hawkins danced the lead
role of the "the First Man" and the remaining eight dancers portrayed animals associated with the Great Plains: an antelope, snake,
hawk, coyote, fish, raccoon, bison, and porcupine.[19] The program
notes for the premiere performance read, "the dance is a ceremony
that takes place on the American plains on one of the days at the
beginning of the world."[20]

More so than his other dances, *Plains Daybreak* has come to exemplify Hawkins' deep synthesis of costumes, masks, and ritual, as well
as his commitment to working collaboratively. Lee discussed
Hawkins' goals in working with costumers and designers:

> [Hawkins] wanted them [the costumes and masks] to be artwork
> that could stand on its own two feet as strongly as the dance
> itself. Especially with a piece like *Plains Daybreak*. I think it was
> true with Ralph Dorazio's sets too. He wanted that to be a work
> of art in itself. That he would look at this proscenium without
> anybody onstage and it would be a beautiful environment, a
> beautiful piece of art. It was partly his rigorous standards that he
> wanted to assert, but at the same time it was a generosity. He
> wanted to make space so the music could be not just things to
> keep the dancers together, but could be a magnificent piece of
> music. So that was one way he would kind of rally all of us who
> worked with him … so he didn't want it to be just for his
> benefit, he wanted it to be for the standards.[21]

The high value Hawkins put on collaboration was aligned with his
effort to create a communal ritualistic event. A practice in which
audiences joined the choreographer, designers, and performers to
engage in a ceremony that honored ideas larger than themselves.
Like Limón's biblical dances, *Plains Daybreak* was an opportunity for
Hawkins' dancers and audiences to experience ritual in a way that
was difficult to find in a secular postwar culture.

From the first dances presented under the auspices of the Erick
Hawkins Dance Company to the end of his career, costumes and
masks played a key role in Hawkins' work.[22] So key were they, that
Hawkins would have the costumes and masks designed and made
before beginning to create the choreography. Hawkins comments,
"my general way is to make the costumes first and then compose the

dance movement around that, so that I mind the possibilities, the specialness of those costumes in that dance."[23] Former Hawkins Company dancers, Laura Pettibone Wright and Catherine Tharin recall the choreographic process for *Plains Daybreak*:

> Hawkins began inventing movement [for *Plains Daybreak*] in September of 1977 after the final revisions of the music, headdresses and costumes were complete. Long tours and conflicts with the dancers delayed moving forward sooner. By the time the choreography began in earnest again during the summer of 1978, many of the original company members had left. Beginning freshly with the new cast, movement was painstakingly developed during hours of rehearsal in heavy headdresses and wool felt costumes.[24]

It was unconventional for a choreographer to give such deep consideration to the ways that costumes and masks might shape the movement vocabulary, partnering, and space. Hawkins' intense and extensive use of masks and costumes was not only crucial to his choreography, but it also played an important role in his theories of embodiment discussed below.

Lee began designing the masks and costumes for *Plains Daybreak* in mid-November 1976 and worked on them on and off until the dance premiered in 1979. The design problems for the masks were twofold, the first was formalist: how to make the masks large enough to read in a theatre, yet light enough to allow the dancers to move fully and freely. The second: how to walk the line between mimeticism, minstrelsy, and abstraction. Although Shawn had stopped performing by the time Hawkins was choreographing *Plains Daybreak*, Shawn's minstrel-based approach in which notions of "authentic costuming" signified authentic connections with Indianness still carried a high value for both performers and audiences.

Compared to Limón, as well as many of his contemporaries, Hawkins' movement vocabulary for *Plains Daybreak* is not complex. There are copious amounts of simple hops and stomping that emphasize the dancers' connection with the earth, a grounded weightiness that was rather uncharacteristic of Hawkins' dances from the 1970s. Usually his dancers skimmed across the stage. For large sections of the dance, the dancers execute movement with knees bent and a torso that is slightly bent to the front, a posture that many reviewers noted as an attribute of Indianness. Other than this forward tilt, the torso is mostly neutral, with little spiraling, curving, or other shaping. Although the dancers occasionally extend a limb, there are few, if any, relationships to the geometrical lines or shapes of the balletic tradition. When coupled with the easeful and non-stressful approach to movement that is the hallmark of the Hawkins style, the dancer's movements convey a "natural" and simple effortlessness.[25]

Like the movement vocabulary, the floor patterns and groupings are also simple. That is, the spatial relationships between the dancers do not feature intricate weavings, level changes, or partnerings. Unlike Limón, Hawkins elides a poly-vocal approach in which dancers perform several different movement phrases or spatial dynamics at once. Hawkins' groupings are done, for the most part, in unison, moving in symmetrical and uncomplicated floor patterns. Dance critics drew on these compositional elements to propose that *Plains Daybreak* was a dance that returned to a ritualistic, pre-modern, or "tribal" dance. The simple movement and uncomplicated groupings pointed to a naïve folksiness and a fantasy of an uncomplicated and harmonious community.

From Graham to *Plains Daybreak*—transformations

In *Martha Graham in Love and War* Mark Franko examines Graham's work between 1938–1953, which he proposes is her most productive period. It is also the period within which Hawkins worked with Graham, 1938–1950. Franko explores Graham's work individually and within the context of her romantic and professional relationship with Hawkins. He also examines Hawkins' choreographic output while with the Graham. Franko argues that Hawkins' most successful dances, while with the Graham Company, were not the dances he choreographed independently, but the solos he choreographed for himself within Graham's dances. Franko writes, "Hawkins' solos within Graham's works are perhaps a more impressive achievement than the solos he did independently during the decade; however they are not recognized as individual achievements because Hawkins did not sign them."[26] Hawkins contributed choreography to some of Graham's most significant and iconic dances, including: *Every Soul is a Circus* (1939), *El Penitente* (1940), *Letter to the World* (1940), *Punch and Judy* (1941), *Deaths and Entrances* (1943), *Appalachian Spring* (1944), *Dark Meadow* (1946), *Cave of the Heart* (1946), *Night Journey*

(1947), and *Eye of Anguish* (1950). Hawkins and Graham's arrange-
ment for choreographic credit was not a unique one in modern
dance. For example, Lucas Hoving, a founding member of the José
Limón Dance Company, also choreographed many of his roles in
Limón's dances, but was not credited.

The last piece Hawkins choreographed while with the Graham
Company, *The Strangler: A Rite of Passage* (1948), was commissioned
by the American Dance Festival and was a solo for Hawkins and
another performer who recited text by Robert Fitzgerald. The title
refers to the legend of Oedipus and the sphinx.[27] Dance reviewers
were overwhelmingly critical of *The Strangler*. Doris Hering's analysis
is exemplary:

> When Erick Hawkins mounts a dance of his own devising, he
> reminds one of a fly caught in a bottle. He buzzes about franti-
> cally bumping his head against all manner of intellectual and the-
> atrical problems and solves them not as the breath-taking dancer
> he could so easily be, but as a silly old professor wearing fly-
> leaves of the Encyclopedia Britannica as blinders.[28]

Hawkins' work with Greek myths predated his association with
Graham, as he graduated from Harvard in 1932 with a major in
Greek Civilization. Graham's interest in Greek myth also predated
her relationship with Hawkins, but once together they joined forces
and dove deeply into mythic narratives and developed what would
become influential theatrical approaches to these ancient texts.
Franko suggests that Hawkins choreographed *The Strangler* in order
to present an alternate version of Graham's *Night Journey*, in which
she interprets Sophocles' *Oedipus Rex* with a focus on Jocasta rather
than Oedipus. Indeed, in several interviews, Hawkins criticized Graham's interpretation of Oedipus Rex as well as her work with Greek
myth in a more general way. Hawkins' central argument was that
Graham used dance to merge her persona with a mythic character as
a vehicle to display her charisma and virtuosity. For Hawkins, it was
a focus on histrionics rather than a more profound and symbolic use
of theatre.

In the DVD, *A Dancer's Life*, Graham discusses the transforma-
tional process she underwent to embody Jocasta in *Night Journey*:

> makeup is a magic, it's a ritual. The means by which you trans-
> form yourself into the character you hope to play. You make up

your face as you think she might have looked. You dress your hair as you think she might have dressed hers. I'm wearing my hair tonight as Jocasta, or at least as I hope she wore it. And then, there comes a moment when she looks at you in the mirror and you realize that she's looking at you and recognizing you as herself.[29]

Through her ritualistic costuming process, in which she strives to mimetically represent Jocasta, Graham is transformed. Her contemporary persona is merged with the ancient Greek myth giving her the grounding on which to merge the personal with the universal. Although Hawkins absorbed Graham's approach to costuming and masks while with her company, once he left, he abandoned her approach and developed new strategies of embodiment.

Openings of the (eye) (1952) was the first dance Hawkins presented after breaking with Graham and although he did not announce it at the time, it was the first dance presented under the auspices of the Erick Hawkins Dance Company.[30] Like *The Strangler, openings of the (eye)* was based on Greek myth and was a solo performed by Hawkins. It featured music by Lucia Dlugoszewski and elaborate costumes and masks by Ralph Dorazio. Hawkins commented that his use of Greek myth in *openings of the (eye)* diverged from Graham's in that he "was using generic, mythic metaphors and not personalized metaphors. And that's where I know it's better [than Graham's]. You see I was using those Greek mythic ideas in their generic terms and not translating them into personal experience."[31] Abandoning what he called Graham's "naturalistic theatre," Hawkins used the artificiality of masks and costumes to reveal the artificiality of theatre. This proved to be a key intervention in the expressionistic performer-audience exchange and a most troubling viewing experience for audiences and critics.

There was not a large group of prewar choreographers engaged in mask work. Rather than masks, Graham, Humphrey, and their colleagues developed the convention of the "neutral modern dance face," which was central to the predominant mode of performer-audience exchange. The purported objectivity of the "neutral modern dance face" foregrounded the expressive potential of the body rather than that of the face, which is so evocative and compelling that it can easily dominate an audience's attention. The "neutral modern dance face" helped to stymie an audience's impulse to identify with the dancer on a personal level and instead focus on the dancer's embodiment of universal themes. Nevertheless, the face was key to completing the audience's viewing of an individual dancer's effort, labor, and control of movement. Dance scholar Sherril Dodds argues that dancers' facial expressions, even if read as neutral, are choreographed according to specific performance conventions. She writes:

> In spite of its neglect, the face participates choreographically in the realization of the aesthetic codes and embodied conventions that pertain to different dance styles and genres. Even a superficial comparison between the intricate facial motilities of a Kathakali dancer and the sexualized facial contortions of Latin American competition dance, or the huge glistening smile of a Broadway chorus girl and the solemn disposition of a Graham performer, indicates that facial expression is not left to chance.[32]

Hawkins found the use of the face limiting. For him, the operation of naturalism in Western theatre fell short of the symbolic use of masks in Eastern theatre. He writes that "over and over people have said. 'What are you hiding behind the mask for?' My answer is that realism and poetry are at odds."[33]

Hawkins' masks gave a face to the unknown and placed the wearer of the mask as the gatekeeper to surreality.[34] In *Plains Daybreak*, Hawkins' masks are symbols of Indianness that allow him to be both his "real" self and a "surreal" someone else. Theatre historian Susan Smith argues that ritualistic masks, such as the ones Hawkins used, announce to the audience that their everyday awareness will be heightened and their quotidian world formalized.[35] Once masked, Hawkins could destabilize his identity and bring ancient figures to the present. By distancing himself once from the audience by his position on stage and a second time by his masks and costumes, Hawkins could direct the focus away from himself and onto symbolic ideas that were more profound than any one individual. As Hawkins writes, a mask, "makes every dance 'sacred,' that is … revealing the big Self instead of the little self."[36]

Original innocence

One of the most productive ways that choreographers used notions of Indianness was to associate themselves with an "original" and "authentic" American body. Native-American cultures provided an original and unmediated lineage through which choreographers could claim an American identity positively, rather than negatively. For example, by integrating notions of an "original" Native-American culture into their dance, choreographers could pronounce that their dance was American, rather than saying what it was not—not European, not Russian, not ballet, or not entertainment. The move was especially productive in the late 1920s and early 30s, as a way to claim a unique American identity that was free from any perceived influence by German modern dance choreographers. Like his predecessors, Hawkins embraced an originary narrative associated with Native-Americans. And more than his other dances that referred to Native-American cultures, *Plains Daybreak* makes copious use of the concept. For example, the program notes for *Plains Daybreak* position it as "a ceremony that takes place on the American plains on one of the days at the beginning of the world." And to underscore the originary premise, Hawkins cast himself as the "First Man" sharing the stage with eight Plains animals. Hawkins' role as "First Man" dancing "at the beginning of the world," situates him within an avant-garde lineage that couples the original, naiveté, and innocence as sources for art. Art critic Rosalind Krauss writes:

> The avant-garde artist has worn many guises over the first hundred years of his existence: revolutionary, dandy, anarchist, aesthete, technologist, mystic. He has also preached a variety of creeds. One thing only seems to hold fairly constant in the vanguardist discourse and that is the theme of originality … More than a rejection or dissolution of the past, avant-garde originality is conceived as a literal origin, a beginning from ground zero, a birth … originality becomes an organicist metaphor referring not so much to formal invention as to sources of life. The self as origin is safe from contamination by tradition because it possesses a kind of originary naiveté.[37]

Hawkins' use of Indianness to construct narratives of an originary moment differed from his predecessors. Hawkins emphasized a naïve innocence as part of this narrative, commenting, "one of the words that's used about my work more than any word is the word innocent. I see it in reviews over and over and over."[38] While Shawn also drew upon notions of innocence to imbue his work with a pre-industrial, "natural," and "pure" quality, Shawn had to navigate the diminutive and infantilizing attributes that also came with innocence. As Deloria argues, there is a long history in which Euro-Americans infantilized Native-Americans, positioning them as, "natural, simple, naïve, preliterate, and devoid of self-consciousness."[39] Shawn's strategy to distance himself from these notions was to perform a hard-hitting and fisted presentation of gender that has been widely recognized as "hyper-masculine." By the time *Plains Daybreak* premiered in 1976, representations of masculinity on the modern dance stage had become more nuanced and the childlike connotations of innocence that Shawn avoided could be welcomed[39]

Geographic and temporal dislocation

Hawkins and the dance writers who discuss his work regularly use geography to create a close association between Hawkins and Native-American cultures. Interviews, articles, and analyses of Hawkins' relationship to Native-American cultures regularly emerge from, or lead to the topic of his birthplace. As Hawkins comments,

> I was born in a little town called Trinidad, Colorado, which is at the very bottom of Colorado. And I can show you exactly how it works. It's the dividing line between the Plains Indian culture and the Southwest Indian culture.[40]

The implication from this oft-repeated narrative is that his birthplace impacted his psyche and spirit so profoundly that he was connected to ways of thinking, feeling, and imagining used by "Indian cultures." This is an easily understood and commonly held narrative. As Radhika Mohanram argues, cultures develop their identity in relation to the land they inhabit. The land shapes "bodies and perceptions, forms their knowledge, and informs their sense of aesthetics."[41] However, the argument for this geographic connection does not acknowledge the colonialist context from which it emerges and operates. It fails to recognize how the United States' geo-political creation of cities, states, and nation have erased the social, political, and cultural land-based practices of indigenous communities. Many of these practices were imperative to Native people's spiritual and cultural communities and integral to an on-going construction of their identities. Hence this failure to recognize colonial-based practices facilitated the Euro-American fantasy of Native-Americans as frozen in a time before contemporary society.[42]

Art historian Caroline Dunant argues that narratives of progress in Western civilization have led contemporary societies to assume that their level of rationality and logic are superior to previous epochs.[43] It is assumed that contemporary societies have "overcome" the emotional, superstitious, and "animal" excesses of the ancients. Deloria discusses this assumption as it applies to Native-American cultures, writing,

> a key mechanism of this temporal dislocation was the notion of progressive cultural evolution: human societies progressed through stages—hunter/gatherer, pastoralist, agriculturalist, trader, manufacturer. Indian people necessarily existed in a different stage and thus, in relation to modern white Americans, in a different temporal zone.[44]

Hawkins engages this temporal dislocation through a complex balancing act of modernist abstraction and notions of ancient Indianness. He and his audiences embraced notions of a refined and sophisticated modernist abstraction as a vehicle to experience an ancient, authentic, and natural Indianness. A process which is examined below.

Postwar autonomy

Since its premiere, *Plains Daybreak* has been lauded as one of Hawkins' seminal and defining works. During the 1980s it was sought after by eager presenting institutions and loved by audiences. Critics positioned *Plains Daybreak* as a highlight of a long career. For example, dance writer Naomi Prevots writes that *Plains Daybreak*:

> is a superb example of Erick Hawkins' latest work. In this dance Hawkins has distilled a lifetime of dance making, and an in-depth look reveals the clarity of his vision and the beauty of his craftsmanship. This dance is one of the most important pieces created by an American choreographer.[45]

While there were those who shared Prevots view, the importance she attributed to Hawkins' dance did not last. *Plains Daybreak* was one of the last vestiges of a representational strategy that endowed Euro-Americans with authorial rights to create work based on a culture other than their own.

After World War II, relegating Indianness to a "natural" and "primitive" past became increasingly complicated. Multicultural agendas and shifts in global relationships blurred racial and nationalist boundaries. As one of the non-white populations who fought in World War II, Native-Americans were slowly receiving acknowledgment for their contributions to the US war efforts and gaining support in their struggle for equality. The Social Darwinism undergirding prewar ideas of race and ethnicity were beginning to give way to a cultural relativism that challenged a singularly dominant Euro-American culture. All of which complicated the ideas of authenticity and primitivity that for so long had been at the core of modern dance's relationship with Indianness.

Notions of multiculturalism and cultural relativity are malleable concepts. While they were used to advance racial equity, they were also used to support notions of an artistic autonomy that gave artists the freedom to engage any cultural heritage, whether it was part of their personal experience or not. As Rosemary Coombe argues, multiculturalism could be seen as a social field of equivalent differences, on which artists were free to incorporate and adapt qualities, attributes, and practices from any culture.[46] In this context, an artist is:

> an autonomous individual who creates fictions with an imagination free of all constraint. For such an author, everything in the world must be made available and accessible as an "idea" that can be transformed into his "expression" which thus becomes his "work." Through his labour, he makes these "ideas" his own; his possession of the "work" is justified by his expressive activity.[47]

This approach to artistic autonomy was not a new postwar creation, it had been embraced by choreographers since the inception of the genre. As Shawn, the "father of modern dance" writes, "the function of the artist is to use authentic themes as seeds from which to produce an art creation of his own."[48] The "authentic themes" to which Shawn was referring were the dances, rituals, and stories of Native-American cultures. To deny Shawn, Hawkins, or their colleagues the right, as authors, to adapt Native-American cultures would have been to deny them their freedom of expression and deprive them of their right to work.

Although both prewar and postwar choreographers claimed artistic autonomy, postwar choreographers faced a new political arena. Rather than the prewar context that was clearly defined by an opposition to fascism and Nazism, postwar choreographers were confronted with a complex set of issues defined by US/Communist relationships. In *Cold War Modernists* Greg Barnhisel discusses this shift, arguing that modernism in the first half of the twentieth-century was an anti-establishment and anti traditionalist search for the new.[49] It was a time when artists broke from previous ideologies of representation and embodiment to develop new movement techniques and choreographic practices. However, after World War II, the strategies for incorporating political and social discourse into artistic productions shifted. For modern dance, a key change was the shift away from political and social concerns and onto formal elements of composition and performance. This prompted audiences to receive *Plains Daybreak* as a poetic abstraction of essences, or a modernist ceremony distilled from Native-American cultures. As Barnhisel argues, it points to the ways that postwar audiences were trained to view "artworks as autonomous aesthetic objects, which prepared them to embrace a depoliticized, aestheticized modernism."[50]

While one can speculate on the ways that Hawkins' audiences recognized the political and cultural systems framing their viewing experience, it is, of course, difficult to grasp these dynamics during the period in which one is living. The questions that *Plains Daybreak* engaged about the political and cultural moment in which Hawkins worked have not been resolved. We are still asking how we can reconcile the purportedly "inauthentic" national self (Hawkins), the underlying "authentic" original ("Indian"), and the actuality of the national modernist dance (American). It is not the low-hanging fruit of "calling out" minstrelsy or cultural appropriation that will move these questions forward, but an ongoing self-examination that addresses the anxieties, guilt, and fear of performing as a national body.

Notes

1 Ide, Leticia. "Dance On." Interview by Billie Mahoney. August 1992.
2 Taliaferro, Clay. "Dance On." Interview by Billie Mahoney. 1981.
3 Rogin, Michael. "Blackface, White Noise: The Jewish Jazz Singer Finds his Voice." *Critical Inquiry*. Vol. 18, No. 3. 1992: 417–453.
4 Deloria, Philip Joseph. *Playing Indian*. Yale University Press, 2007.
5 "Erick Hawkins Offers *Plains Daybreak.*" *New York Times*. February 9, 1983.
6 Manning, Susan. *Modern Dance, Negro Dance: Race in Motion*. Minneapolis: University of Minnesota Press, 2004.
7 Manning, Susan. *Modern Dance, Negro Dance: Race in Motion*. Minneapolis: University of Minnesota Press, 2004.

8 Manning, Susan. *Modern Dance, Negro Dance: Race in Motion*. Minneapolis: University of Minnesota Press, 2004.
9 Hawkins, Erick. "Why Does a Man Dance, And What Does He Dance, And Who Should Watch Him?" In *The Dance Experience; Readings in Dance Appreciation*, edited by Myron Nadel and Constance Nadel. New York: Praeger, 1970.
10 Lloyd, Harold. Interview. 1971.
11 Humphrey quoted in Cohen, Selma Jean. *Doris Humphrey: An Artist First, An Autobiography*. Middleton, CT: Wesleyan University Press, 1972.
12 Hering, Doris. "José Limón: Midstream Vintage Years in Retrospect." *Dance Magazine*. November 1973: 42–47.
13 Lloyd quoted in Cohen, Selma Jean. *Doris Humphrey: An Artist First, An Autobiography*. Middleton, CT: Wesleyan University Press, 1972.
14 Lloyd, Margaret. "José Limón." In *The Borzoi Book of Modern Dance*. New York: A. A. Knopf, 1949.
15 Johnston, Jill. *Marmalade Me*. New York: Dutton, 1971.
16 Limón, José and Lynn Garafola. *José Limón: An Unfinished Memoir*. Hanover, NH: University Press of New England, 1998.
17 See Murphy, Jacqueline Shea. *The People Have Never Stopped Dancing: Native American Modern Dance Histories*. University of Minnesota Press, 2007.
18 Shawn, Ted. *The American Ballet*. H. Holt and Company, 1926.
19 The original 1979 cast featured: First Man, Erick Hawkins; Raccoon, Laura Pettibone; Snake, Helen Pelton; Buffalo, Douglas Andresen; Fish, Cynthia Reynolds; Antelope, Mark Wisniewski; Coyote, Randy Howard; Porcupine, Daniel Tai; Hawk, Cathy Ward.
20 Kisselgoff, Anna. "Creation of the World by Hawkins." In *7 Essays on the Dance of Erick Hawkins*. New York: Foundation for Modern Dance, 1982.
21 Lee, Ralph. Interview by Caroline Sutton Clark. 2010.
22 In *openings of the (eye)* Hawkins worked closely with Dorazio to create multiple masks and costumes, a mask and costume for each of the five sections of the dance: *Discovery of the Minotaur, Disconsolate Chimera, Ritual of the Descent, Goat of the God, and Eros the Firstborn*.
23 Hawkins quoted in Pennella, Florence. "The Vision of Erick Hawkins." *Dance Scope*. September 1953.
24 Wright, Laura and Catherine Tharin. *Plains Daybreak*. 2018.
25 As I discussed in Chapter 2, Hawkins' use of this facile and released movement style was an updating of the dichotomy between Euro-American training and "primitive" bodies.
26 Franko, Mark. *Martha Graham in Love and War: The Life in the Work*. Oxford University Press, 2014.
27 Hawkins also included his own program note:

   The SPHINX, half lion and half woman, represents the father and mother in the primal scene, her wings are a symbol of the physical ecstasy of the parents, and her name, in Greek meaning the Strangler, refers to the dancer of parental fixation or domination.

OIDIPOUS overcomes the Sphinx by discerning in her the child's phantasy of the primal scene and by deciphering her riddle to mean the four-legged being of the primal scene, the two-legged image of the naked human being, and the three-legged image of the physically creative man. His name in Greek is a euphemism, Swollen Foot.

(Hawkins quoted in Anderson, 13)

28 Hering quoted in "An American Dance Festival." *Dance Magazine*, October 1948, Anderson, Jack. *The American Dance Festival*. Durham: Duke University Press, 1987.
29 Graham quoted in "A Dancer's World." Martha Graham. Dir. Peter Glushanok. 1957.
30 *Openings of the (eye)* consisted of five sections: *Discovery of the Minotaur, Disconsolate Chimera, Ritual of the Descent, Goat of the God, and Eros the Firstborn*.
31 Hawkins, Erick. Interview by David Sears. June 9, 1985.
32 Dodds, Sherril. "The Choreographic Interface: Dancing Facial Expression in Hip Hop and Neo-Burlesque Striptease." *Dance Research Journal*. Vol. 46, No. 2. 2014: 38–55. 39.
33 Hawkins, Erick. "Erick Hawkins on Masks." *Mime, Mask, and Marionette*. Summer, 1978: 106–113.
34 Smith, Susan. *Masks in Modern Drama*. University of California Press, 1984.
35 Smith, Susan. *Masks in Modern Drama*. University of California Press, 1984.
36 Hawkins quoted in Sorell, Walter. *The Other Face: The Mask in the Arts*. London: Thames and Hudson. 1973. 157.
37 Krauss, Rosalind. *October*. Vol. 18. Autumn, 1981: 47–66.
38 Deloria, Philip Joseph. *Playing Indian*. Yale University Press, 2007.
39 Hawkins, Erick. Interview by David Sears. May 27, 1983.
40 Hawkins, Erick. Interview by David Sears. December 10, 1982.
41 Mohanram, Radhika. *Black Body: Women, Colonialism, and Space*. Minneapolis: University of Minnesota Press, 1999.
42 Deloria, Philip Joseph. *Playing Indian*. Yale University Press, 2007. 276.
43 Dunant, Caroline. "Olympian Dreamscapes: The Photographic Canvas. The Wide-Screen Paintings of Leighton, Poynter and Alma Tadema." In *Melodrama: Stage, Picture Screen*, edited by Jacky Bratton, Jim Cook, and Christine Gledhill. London: BFI, 1994.
44 Deloria, Philip Joseph. *Playing Indian*. Yale University Press, 2007. 106.
45 Prevots, Naomi. "Erick Hawkins: Redefining America." In *7 Essays on the Dance of Erick Hawkins*. Foundation for Modern Dance, 1982.
46 Coombe, Rosemary. "The Properties of Culture and the Politics of Possessing Identity: Native Claims in the Cultural Appropriation Controversy." In *Canadian Journal of Law and Jurisprudence*. 1993: 249–285.
47 Coombe, Rosemary. "The Properties of Culture and the Politics of Possessing Identity: Native Claims in the Cultural Appropriation Controversy." In *Canadian Journal of Law and Jurisprudence*. 1993: 249–285.
48 Shawn, Ted. *The American Ballet*. H. Holt and Company, 1926. 20.
49 Barnhisel, Greg. *Cold War Modernists*. Columbia University Press, 2015.
50 Barnhisel, Greg. *Cold War Modernists*. Columbia University Press, 2015.

Works cited

A Dancer's World. Martha Graham. Dir. Peter Glushanok. 1957.

Anderson, Jack. *The American Dance Festival*. Durham, NC: Duke University Press, 1987. 41.

Barnhisel, Greg. *Cold War Modernists*. New York: Columbia University Press, 2015.

Coombe, Rosemary. "The Properties of Culture and the Politics of Possessing Identity: Native Claims in the Cultural Appropriation Controversy." *Canadian Journal of Law and Jurisprudence*. 1993: 249–285.

Deloria, Philip Joseph. *Playing Indian*. New Haven, CT: Yale University Press, 2007. 106.

Dodds, Sherril. "The Choreographic Interface: Dancing Facial Expression in Hip Hop and Neo-Burlesque Striptease." *Dance Research Journal*. Vol. 46, No. 2. 2014: 38–55.

Dunant, Caroline. "Olympian Dreamscapes: The Photographic Canvas. The Wide-Screen Paintings of Leighton, Poynter and Alma Tadema." In *Melodrama: Stage, Picture Screen*, edited by Jacky Bratton, Jim Cook, and Christine Gledhill. London: BFI, 1994.

Franko, Mark. *Martha Graham in Love and War: The Life in the Work*. New York: Oxford University Press, 2014: 84.

Hawkins, Erick. "Erick Hawkins on Masks." *Mime, Mask, and Marionette*. Summer. 1978: 106–113.

Hawkins, Erick. Interview by David Sears. December 10, 1982.

Hawkins, Erick. Interview by David Sears. May 27, 1983.

Hawkins, Erick. Interview by David Sears. June 9, 1985.

Hawkins, Erick. "Why Does a Man Dance, And What Does He Dance, And Who Should Watch Him?" *The Dance Experience; Readings in Dance Appreciation*, edited by Myron Nadel and Constance Nadel. New York: Praeger, 1970.

Hering quoted in "An American Dance Festival." *Dance Magazine*, October 1948.

Hering, Doris. "José Limón: Midstream Vintage Years in Retrospect." *Dance Magazine*. November 1973: 42–47.

Humphrey quoted in Cohen, Selma Jean. *Doris Humphrey: An Artist First, An Autobiography*. Middleton, CT: Wesleyan University Press, 1972.

Ide, Leticia. "Dance On." Interview by Billie Mahoney. August 1992.

Johnston, Jill. *Marmalade Me*. New York: Dutton, 1971.

Kisselgoff, Anna. "Erick Hawkins Offers *Plains Daybreak*." *New York Times*. February 9, 1983.

Kisselgoff, Anna. "Creation of the World by Hawkins." In *7 Essays on the Dance of Erick Hawkins*. New York: Foundation for Modern Dance, 1982.

Krauss, Rosalind. *October*. Vol. 18. Autumn, 1981: 47–66.

Lee, Ralph. Interview by Caroline Sutton Clark. 2010.

Limón, José and Lynn Garafola. *José Limón: An Unfinished Memoir*. Hanover, NH: University Press of New England, 1998.

Lloyd, Harold. Interview. 1971

Lloyd, Margaret. "José Limón." In *The Borzoi Book of Modern Dance*. New York: A. A. Knopf, 1949.

Manning, Susan. *Modern Dance, Negro Dance: Race in Motion*. Minneapolis, MN: University of Minnesota Press, 2004.

Mohanram, Radhika. *Black Body: Women, Colonialism, and Space*. Minneapolis, MN: University of Minnesota Press, 1999.

Murphy, Jacqueline Shea. *The People Have Never Stopped Dancing: Native American Modern Dance Histories*. Minneapolis, MN: University of Minnesota Press, 2007.

Pennella, Florence. "The Vision of Erick Hawkins." *Dance Scope*. September 1953.

Prevots, Naomi. "Erick Hawkins: Redefining America." In *7 Essays on the Dance of Erick Hawkins*, edited by Anna Kisselgoff et al. New York: Foundation for Modern Dance, 1982.

Rogin, Michael. "Blackface, White Noise: The Jewish Jazz Singer Finds his Voice." *Critical Inquiry*. Vol. 18, No. 3. 1992: 417–453.

Selma Jean. *Doris Humphrey: An Artist First, An Autobiography*. Middleton, CT: Wesleyan University Press, 1972.

Shawn, Ted. *The American Ballet*. New York: H. Holt and Company, 1926.

Smith, Susan. *Masks in Modern Drama*. Berkeley, CA: University of California Press, 1984.

Sorell, Walter. *The Other Face: The Mask in the Arts*. London: Thames and Hudson, 1973.

Taliaferro, Clay. "Dance On." Interview by Billie Mahoney. 1981.

Wright, Laura and Catherine Tharin. "Erick Hawkins' Collaborations in the Choreographing of Plains Daybreak." *Dance: Current Selected Research*. Vol. 9. 2018.

Chapter 4

Brown in black and white
José Limón dances
The Emperor Jones

In a discussion on the Humphrey/Limón dance technique, former Limón School Director, Alan Danielson comments,

> the original people that danced with him [Limón] Betty Jones, Ruth Currier, and Lucas Hoving, they would always say, no it's not a technique, it's not a style, it's a philosophy. And it is, it's a way of thinking of dancing the human being.[1]

For Limón, a queer brown man, "dancing the human being" involved a different set of concerns than those engaged by his Euro-American colleagues. His solutions to performing humanity within modern dance conventions that delineated how humanity was expressed and who could express it, proved to be innovative and influential. This chapter explores how Limón's "dance of the human" complicated the raced and gendered borders that circum-navigated his queer brown body.

As Susan Manning has argued, Limón's culturally marked or unmarked status within modern dance's racial continuum could shift, depending on the particular dance he performed.[2] In the many reviews of Limón's choreography and performances, writers either made no comment about his race, which positioned him as culturally unmarked, or made racially based descriptions that marked him as Mexican, Spanish, Indian, Aztec, or Latin. This chapter explores Limón's multiple cultural identities through his 1956 dance, *The Emperor Jones*, based on Eugene O'Neill's play of the same name. My analysis of this dance revolves around Limón's choice to put himself and his all-male cast in black body paint. Former Limón Company member Peter Sparling recalls, "usually that [*The Emperor Jones*] was programmed as the last piece because all the men had to rub themselves with Eddy Leonard black makeup ... entirely covering ourselves with black makeup, we'd even spray our hair, the fair-haired guys."[3, 4] O'Neill's play tells the story of Brutus Jones, an African-American Pullman porter who escapes from a chain gang to a "West Indies" island. Once there, he tricks the local "natives" into thinking that only a silver bullet can kill him and with this symbolic power, quickly makes himself emperor. By the play's end, Jones is shot and killed by silver bullets especially prepared by the "native rebels."

Contextualized within modern dance's black/white racial binary, Limón's painted body incorporated three bodies; a brown Mexican body; a white "American" body (with the privilege to represent the Other); and the black body of Brutus Jones.[5] Limón's tripled body could be read in a number of ways. Audiences could use Limón's Mexican-Americaness to differentiate him from both white and black bodies. Alternatively, Limón could be read as a body with white privilege who was different from black bodies, or Limón could also share the non-whiteness of black bodies thus, different from white bodies. Depending on an audience member's reading of Limón as the same or different from themselves and other audience members, they could feel they were participating in a cultural event that constructed racial diversity. So, while it could be argued that Limón's tripled body expanded racialized boundaries and diversified mid-century US modern dance, its operation within and alignment with predominant conventions for staging race could not break down or synthesize the modern dance's prevailing black/white racial binary. Again, as Manning has argued, Limón's performances as both a culturally marked and unmarked body upheld the black/white binary and status quo of racial conventions in mid-century US modern dance.[6]

In addition to exploring how Limón's tripled body revealed the resilience of racialized conventions in modern dance, this chapter also examines how *The Emperor Jones* acted as a framework for Limón's construction of non-normative homosocial spaces. As the author will argue, the performance of Limón and his all-male cast in *The Emperor Jones* has proven to be one of his most complex responses to narratives of race, heteronormative desire, and mid-century homophobic anxieties.

US modern dance and minstrelsy

Limón's use of black paint in *The Emperor Jones* was an anomalous event in postwar modern dance. Although the generation of

Euro-American modern dancers prior to Limón referred to African-American practices, music, and rituals, they did not use black paint.[7] Instead, they created choreographic metaphors, what Susan Manning terms *metaphorical minstrelsy*, a performance convention whereby white modern dancers did not mimic others, but "presented an abstraction or personification of others."[8] Notable examples of metaphorical minstrelsy include Helen Tamaris's *Negro Spirituals* and Ted Shawn's *Four Dances Based on American Folk Music*. However, Tamiris performed her *Negro Spirituals* for the last time in 1944 and Shawn disbanded his company in 1940.[9] By the mid-1950s, when Limón debuted *The Emperor Jones*, metaphorical minstrelsy had been abandoned by European-American dancers and self-representations by African-American modern dance choreographers were steadily growing. This makes Limón's decision to use black paint and its acceptance by critics and audiences all the more inexplicable.

Unlike Euro-American blackface minstrels before him, Limón did not use black paint as a vehicle to ridicule African-Americans. Rather than a degrading impersonation of a generalized African-American "type," Limón used black paint as a way to keep the dance "true" to O'Neill's story within a naturalistic theatrical tradition that had yet to explore color blind casting. Limón connected to O'Neill's narrative through a movement vocabulary that combined mimetic and abstract modes intended to communicate the purported universal themes in O'Neill's text. Limón's mimetic mode, which included gestural movement, set pieces, and costuming, were used to establish O'Neill's narrative and characters. Once established, Limón abstracted movement, spatial relationships, and groupings of dancers to present the emotional and psychological states of Brutus Jones.

The performing of racial difference through representation had been a distinctly Euro-American privilege. Brenda Dixon-Gottschild examines the performer-audience relationship in Euro-Americans performance of blackface minstrelsy. She argues that the representation of blackness that Euro-American blackface minstrels' performed pivoted on the audience's awareness that the minstrels were not black, but only wearing signs of blackness that they could put on and take off.[10] The highly stylized way Euro-American blackface minstrels painted their faces underscored the fact that they were wearing a mask. It allowed Euro-American blackface minstrels to say, "[t]his is a character—not *me*. I am playing a role here."[11] This gave Irish-American and Jewish-American immigrants, the two groups making the most extensive use of blackface, an avenue to displace their anxieties about assimilation onto African-Americans.[12] By "blacking up," these minstrels diminished their own marginalized histories through the even more marginalized bodies of African-Americans

This management of racial hierarchies is seen in both O'Neill and Limón's production of *The Emperor Jones*. At different historical periods and in different contexts, both O'Neill and Limón were racially marginalized and disenfranchised. O'Neill as an Irish man in the early part of the twentieth-century, when the Irish were regularly denied privileges and opportunities experienced by dominant Northern European groups; and Limón as a Mexican at mid-century, when the US government implemented practices to differentiate and oppress Mexicans and Mexican-Americans.[13] From the signing of the 1848 Treaty of Guadalupe Hidalgo, when US territory expanded to include land previously held by Mexico, Mexican-American's "racial" status has shifted depending on context, time, and place.[14]

Premiered by the Provincetown Players at the Playwrights Theatre in 1920, O'Neill's production of *The Emperor Jones* did not use black body paint, as was the practice of the day. Instead O'Neill cast the African-American actor Charles Gilpin in the lead role of Brutus Jones. By casting Gilpin, rather than a white actor in blackface, O'Neill intervened in the then dominant performance conventions of minstrelsy. However, by situating Jones's black body as a discursive site representing a primitivist caricature of blackness, O'Neill also perpetuated representational strategies undergirding the performance of minstrelsy. While the complexities and contradictions at play in these representational machinations could easily upend a play's reception, they did not impede the success of O'Neill's work. On the contrary, these tensions contributed to *The Emperor Jones's* huge triumph and put O'Neill on the theatrical map. As Shannon Steen has argued, O'Neill's rise to prominence and his contribution to the legitimizing of American theatre came, in large part, through the racialized and sexualized spectacle of the black body.[15]

Dancing about race and not dancing about race

Limón's original all-male cast for *The Emperor Jones* featured Limón as Brutus Jones; Lucas Hoving as Smithers, whom Limón credits as "The White Man;" and six company members performing the two alternating roles of "The Emperor's Subjects" and "The Little Form-less Fears." Limón's dance follows O'Neill's text in a loose way, broadening the scope of some characters and scenes, while diminishing others, an approach Limón established in *The Moor's Pavane* (1949), and continued to refine throughout his career. Like his other story-ballets of the 1950s, the choreographic structure of *The Emperor Jones* consists of a series of solos and duets danced by Limón and Hoving interspersed with sections of group dancing.

The Emperor Jones is a fine example of how Limón adapted the often stark and fragmented movement vocabularies and minimalist groupings of prewar choreographers into a more lyrical, multi-level, and polyvocal presentation. He transformed Humphrey's highly personal movement vocabulary by adding body isolations, fluidity of carving through space, and more robust sequencing through the body. Additionally, Limón's spatial arrangements of groups engaged the stage in more dynamic ways by covering more space and performing longer movement phrases. He also increased the use of levels through jumps, lifts, and floorwork. Taken together, Limón's augmentations of Humphrey's work made his groupings more complex in the sense that there were more weavings, a greater dynamic range, increased level changes, and contrapuntal phrases.

The Emperor Jones' original cast members were the last generation of Limón dancers who lacked extensive ballet training. Although Limón had begun teaching at Juilliard in 1951, his 1954 company was not yet dominated by Juilliard alumni.[16] Limón Dance Company alumna Sarah Stackhouse comments, "[t]hat particular group of men of which those dances [*The Emperor Jones* and *The Traitor*] were choreographed were very powerful and wild dancers. They hadn't learned to tame their movement into proper pirouettes."[17] In a way, Limón and Hawkins act as bookends to modern dance's relationship with ballet. Hawkins played a central role in introducing ballet technique into the Graham Company, which, due to Graham's dominance at that time, spread through the genre and spurred the development of a more versatile and technically efficient modern dancer. On the other end, Limón was the first modern dance choreographer whose work was licensed by ballet companies, which promoted the trend for a higher degree of expressivity in ballet dancers. Although Humphrey and Limón's prewar approach to dance was strongly defined by their ideological and technical opposition to ballet, Limón's use of narrative and musicality in his story ballets created an unexpected alignment. The performance rights to

The Traitor and *The Moor's Pavane* were sold to American Ballet Theatre in 1969 and that same year, The Royal Swedish Ballet presented an all-Limón program.

While it is clear that Limón's formalist methods for choreography emerged from his long and prosperous association with Humphrey, *The Emperor Jones* had cinematic influences as well. Limón Dance Company alumnus Daniel Lewis comments on the impact the 1933 film, *The Emperor Jones*, starring Paul Robeson, made on Limón. Lewis comments:

> So, I had asked him [Limón] if he had seen the movie and he sort of smiled and looked at me. Of course he'd seen the film ... He took a great play which he read first, saw this film which had an influence on it [the dance] because Paul Robeson was incredible as the Emperor Jones in that film and José emulated a lot of the spirit that Robeson had in the film in his choreography. And costumes and sets and all that went along with it.[18]

The film of *The Emperor Jones* and Robeson's highly acclaimed portrayal of Brutus Jones owed much to Robeson's powerful physical presence. From the first scene, Robeson gives Brutus Jones a bravura, confidence, and swagger that sets up a dynamic contrast to Jones' psychological break down that occurs later in the play. Many of Robeson's larger-than-life posturings and presentational manners can be seen in Limón's performance. Similarities can also be seen in Limón's stylization of costumes. Like Robeson, Limón costumes himself in military regalia. His jacket features large epaulettes, broad cuffs, and is designed to make his chest appear broad. His pants are three-quarter length and he wears glittering gold boots. His hat is wide-brimmed and sports a large feather. The military styling of this costuming signifies a violence and strength that gives Jones the power and credibility analogous to that of a white heterosexual commander. However, the costume can also be read as extreme or flamboyant. It can be seen as a gaudy and over-the-top representation of military authority that reveals Jones' insecurity, inadequacy, and marginality. O'Neill sums up Jones's posturing by writing: "[y]et there is something not altogether ridiculous about his grandeur. He has a way of carrying it off."[19] Although Jones can "carry it off," his grandeur is somewhat ridiculous, not simply because he is attempting to embody the grandeur of an emperor, but because he attempts to embody a grandeur typically assigned to white bodies.

Aoife Monks argues that Jones first internalizes a way of performing whiteness during his time as a Pullman Porter.[20] In the first scene of *The Emperor Jones*, Jones tells Smithers,

> [f]or de little stealin' dey gits you in jail soon or late. For de big stealin' dey makes you Emperor ... If dey's one thing I learns in ten years on de Pullman ca's listenin' to de white quality talk, it's dat same fact. And when I gits a chance to use it I winds up Emperor in two years.[21]

Although Jones does become emperor, his performance as a white authoritarian proves to be short-lived. As Shannon Steen argues, the ultimate tragedy in *The Emperor Jones* is Jones's insupportable social position in which he is "too black to succeed in America and too white (in terms of his oppressive policies as Emperor) to sustain his regime on the island."[22] Although Jones' performances of whiteness allows him to maneuver his way to the Emperor's throne, the performance is unsustainable.

Like Jones, Limón was a kind of emperor. In her memorial to Limón upon his passing, Deborah Jowitt writes, "José Limón was the King, and we, his fervent subjects, tried to dance and to think about dance the way we thought he would have wanted us to."[23] However, unlike Jones' short-lived racial border crossing, Limón's tenure as a leading voice in modern dance was long and prosperous. Limón was able to consistently cross and straddle non-white/white borders from 1929, when he began working with the Humphrey/Weidman Dance Company, to the end of his career in 1972. And although there were non-white dancers and choreographers contemporaneous with Limón who also crossed and straddled racialized borders in mid-century US modern dance, none did so as consistently and at the high level that Limón realized.

Limón's mid-century "empire" was bounded by the ongoing tensions between formalist concerns and social and political issues. From its premiere at the prestigious Empire State Music Festival, *The Emperor Jones'* high-art framing kept it at arm's length from critical reflections on race. With the dance based on O'Neill's text, a leading American playwright and music from Heitor Villa-Lobos, a leading international composer, Limón's dance was firmly situated as an elite cultural production that transcended racial issues. Reviews elided race and instead focused on the performance qualities of Limón and Hoving's dancing. Doris Hering discussed the ways that Limón and

Hoving's "strengths made one overlook occasional moments of muddled choreography."[24] when the dance was re-staged for a new cast at the 1972 American Dance Festival, critics did not write about why, 16 years after *The Emperor Jones'* premiere, and after the many victories of the Civil Rights Movement, the Limón dancers still wore black paint. Instead, they once more focused on formalist values and performances qualities. Dance critic Jack Anderson writes that the Limón Company:

> took a great risk, for ... [*The Emperor Jones*] ... had originally been acclaimed not so much for the ingenuity or expressiveness of its formal design (which could be preserved in a revival) as for the powerful performances of Limón ... and Hoving.[25]

This formalist-based reception was radically different from O'Neill's when he premiered *The Emperor Jones* in 1920. While reviewers discussed formalist production values of the play and praised O'Neill's ingenuity and originality, there were also heated discussions around O'Neill's choice to cast the African-American actor Charles Gilpin as Jones rather than a Euro-American actor in blackface. The critics who discussed Gilpin's performance regularly positioned his performance as "natural," in the sense that his African heritage endowed him with essentialized "gifts" to portray Jones. The notion that Gilpin was a disciplined and highly skilled theatre artist was rarely discussed.[26] These essentialist readings, as well as issues of minstrelsy as a performance strategy, remained a troubling and reoccurring part *The Emperor Jones'* theatre history as it was restaged throughout the twentieth and twenty-first centuries.[27]

A striking exception, perhaps the singular exception, to the formalist-based reviews of *The Emperor Jones* came from Poland. In a 1958 article that Limón wrote for *Dance Observer*, he discusses the reaction of a Polish government official who, after seeing *The Emperor Jones* as part of a Limón Dance Company tour, asked Limón if he had been permitted to perform the dance in the US. The Polish official could not understand how the racial issues embedded in *The Emperor Jones* could be overlooked by US audiences, especially in light of the recent high-profile incident of racial school segregation in Arkansas, when the "Little Rock Nine" were prevented from entering a white high school by Arkansas' Governor. Limón's reply to the Polish official was that "*Emperor Jones* was first of all a work of art, and I hoped a good one, and that even if it were in defiance of prevalent political and social usages, no one would or could prohibit its performance."[28] As Rebekah Kowal has discussed, Limón's tour to Poland was sponsored by the US State Department as part of an effort to, "demonstrate the superiority of American artistic ingenuity, the seriousness of artistic pursuit, and the autonomy of the artist under a capitalist democracy."[29] And as I discussed in Chapter 4, it was the United States' State Department's strategy that Limón's work would reveal the "superiority" of his "freedom" under a capitalist democracy and provide a convincing response to critics of US race relations.

Styling race

By the time Limón choreographed *The Emperor Jones* in 1956, his apprenticeship under and collaboration with Doris Humphrey had produced a movement vocabulary and technique that was recognized as the Humphrey/Limón style and technique. Although Limón's adaptations and modifications to Humphrey's approaches had altered her technique, the key expressionistic goal of using movement to bring the inside to the outside remained intact. Contextualizing Limón's choreography for *The Emperor Jones* within this stylistic tradition, we can see Jones' demise from the white subjectivity of the emperor to an essentialized black body is represented by Jones' inability to express his interior world.

The dance opens with Jones sitting on his throne while the corps dancers enter to perform a group section. This is followed by a solo for Jones. Throughout these opening sections, Jones is in control of his movements and is able to express his complex persona as Emperor. However, as the dance continues, Jones' control over movements gradually fade. He begins to lumber, shake, and stumble through his world, losing the ability to express the emotions that he embodies. His inability to use dance's expressionist language to communicate his emotions reveals the irrationality purportedly inherent in his non-white body. It becomes apparent that his performance of whiteness, which had allowed him to transcend his black body and become emperor, is failing.

There is one movement in particular that exemplifies this non-whiteness, what I call "torso wiggles." The torso wiggles are big shudders that run through Jones's body, a kind of involuntary shaking that Jones unexpectedly experiences. They sometimes appear to be aftershocks of something troubling that happened to him that we couldn't see and that he does not understand. The torso wiggles represent things happening to Jones that he cannot control, as if he is experiencing internal spasms that he is unable to hide or stylize. These unrefined, pedestrian and raw movements would come to be used extensively by subsequent generations of modern dance and jazz choreographers, but in the context of the Humphrey/Limón movement tradition, the torso wiggles signify something that is random, unformed, and unaccounted for. It was outside of the Euro-American style of expression.

Limón also makes ample use of weight to stylize Jones' character. From the opening of the dance, Limón gives Jones a weighted gravitas. Jones is able to "throw his weight around" to get what he wants. In keeping with the arc of O'Neill's narrative, Jones's ability to control and direct the strength and power of his weight deteriorates as the dance progresses. The sure, stable, and broad physical attitude that Jones begins with gradually becomes strained. Rather than keeping the movement of his arms and legs integrated with his center, which allows for efficient and facile movement, Jones extends his reach beyond what he can bear or control. The further Jones extends his movements from the center of his body, the more energy he needs to control his movement, resulting in an uncontrolled and mismanaged expenditure of energy. Rather than choosing to move of his own volition, Jones is forced to move. The world of white privilege is beyond his grasp and his attempts to reach it paint him as excessive and irrational.

Staging homosociality and heterosexual desire

Dance scholar Ramsay Burt has shown how the feminization of male dancers through their position as an object rather than subject of the gaze was and is central to the staging of gender in US modern dance and ballet.[30] Burt argues that the traditional male/female ballet *pas de deux* facilitates viewing practices that situate the two dancers' intimate body contact within normalized narratives of heteronormative desire. Within this configuration, the male ballet dancer normalizes his masculinity and gains agency and subjectivity by deflecting the audience's gaze onto the female dancer. Unlike the ballerina, he does not acknowledge the male spectator's gaze, but serves as the representative of that gaze in objectifying the female dancer. Through bodily postures, movements, and spatial relationships with the ballerina the male ballet dancer sutures his gaze to the gaze of male audience members in viewing the ballerina, which helps to construct his subjectivity.

While this traditional tactic worked for male dancers in gender-mixed casts, male choreographers presenting all-male casts had to find new approaches. A tactic that Limón's prominent precursor, Ted Shawn, regularly used was to choreograph unison movement. If Shawn's all-male casts were performing the same movement vocabulary and same spatial patterns at the same time, they would not come into physical contact with each other. As Susan Foster, Susan Manning, and Julia Foulkes have discussed, the exception to Shawn's "no touching" strategy were times when the entire cast converged to create a single grouping.[31] These groupings were usually a culminating point in the dance and it was not uncommon for a single dancer to be lifted upward toward an idealized space. The unified designs and singular focus of the dancers neutralized any one-to-one relationships between men within the group. Their unity and focus tell us that they are not there to interact with each other individually, but to communally support—literally and figuratively—a spiritual or idealized ascension. During these groupings it was possible for typically taboo body contact to be made between the dancer's groins, buttocks, torsos, and faces. However, since this contact served a community in pursuit of a spiritual, athletic, or idealized notion, it achieved a heteronormative framing. Same-sex touching in Shawn's dances was usually done within these larger groupings. If touching of illicit body parts was made in smaller groupings of duets or trios they could more easily represent an explicitly non-normative homosexual pairing.

Shawn combined this "only group touching" policy with an almost exclusive use of hard, strong, and athletic movements intended to associate himself and his dancers with masculinity and clearly disassociate them from movement coded as queer or feminine. As Walter Terry writes:

> When I was first starting to dance and Ted Shawn first began, all the men used fists most of the time … the classical ballet, the port de bras, was something that looked effeminate … the convention of the hand, convention of the deportment, instead of seeming gentlemanly, seemed effeminate to people that were hacking down trees and building log cabins and fighting Indians and plowing the soil and freezing to death in New England.[32]

The notion of the All-American frontiersman held a deeply entrenched position within the cultural imaginary. Representations of masculinity traded on a rough-and-tumble pioneering spirit, which meant that the aura of artistic refinement was a notion for the male dancer to avoid. Shawn's fisted gestures helped shield him from perceptions that his dancing was a refined and elite artistic expression. Shawn's fisted vocabulary promoted the reading that his dancers were fighters and laborers whose dance was action, not art and fighting, not design.

Limón's choreography for *The Emperor Jones* expanded significantly on Shawn's approaches. *The Emperor Jones* was Limón's fourth dance featuring an all-male cast, all of which received significant choreographic contributions from Lucas Hoving, a founding member of the José Limón Dance Company.[33] By the time *The Emperor Jones* was choreographed in 1956, Limón and Hoving had developed a powerful collaborative process through which they choreographed same-sex duets that tested and resisted previous conventions of partnering and gender regulations. There were no other male duets in mid-century modern dance that claimed such a central position within a dance and lasted for such an extended period of time. Indeed, to find male/female duets in mid-century dance, that played a comparable role within a dance, one would have to look to the male/female *pas de deux* of classical ballet.[34] US modern dance audiences would not see the intense intimacy of Limón and Hoving's same-sex partnering again until the work of Bill T. Jones and Arnie Zane in the early 1980s.

As in Limón's previous all-male dances, *The Emperor Jones* made extensive use of violence to stage relationships between men. The hostile qualities of his choreography offered audiences a way to manage their homoerotic anxiety by focusing on the dancer's violent physical prowess and dramatic expressiveness rather than possible erotic relationships within an all-male cast. In O'Neill's play, the character of Smithers appears only briefly at the beginning and end of the play to set up and close down what is an otherwise one-man play. Limón's adaptation transforms Smithers, danced by Hoving, into the more archetypal "The White Man." And rather than brief appearances at the beginning and end of the play, Limón puts The White Man on stage throughout most of the dance as Jones' nemesis who Limón engages in a series of duets-as-fights.

Limón's use of space and floor patterns in these duets figure prominently in both heightening and assuaging anxieties over same-sex partnering. The duets do not stay in one place for long. For the most part, they travel through space, often with Limón and Hoving carrying or dragging each other. Duets that travel bring attention to traveling, while duets that are more spatially static prompt audience members to focus more closely on the intimate and possibly sexualized physical partnering between the dancers. Duets that travel direct the audience's attention away from Limón and Hoving's intimate connection to the larger stage space and choreographic formations. This helps audiences situate Limón and Hoving within more normative narratives of sexuality and masculinity. However, locomoting through space does not entirely or always obfuscate non-normative readings. Limón and Hoving's partnering and illicit body contact queered the space, offering opportunities for non-normative readings of marginalized identities.

In addition to these duets-as-fights, Limón also drew on the violence of gun culture embedded in O'Neill's play. As mentioned in the brief synopsis of the play at the beginning of this chapter, Jones' rises to power occurred through his deception that only a silver bullet can kill him. This deception happens in the first act of the play and from that point to the end, guns are integral to the motion of the plot forward. O'Neill biographer Travis Bogard writes that before settling on *The Emperor Jones* as a title, O'Neill used *The Silver Bullet*, which was "an indication of the importance of the bullet in the play's design. Jones's bullet is his emperorhood epitomized in a single destructive symbol; it is his talisman, his rabbit's foot, his fate."[35] This interpretation was not lost on Limón. Costumed with a pistol in a holster belted around his waist, Limón used guns to imbue Jones with a violent sexuality and self-destructiveness.

Richard King argues that gun culture is dominated by a male homosociality that operates through heterosexual economies of misogyny and masculinity. He underscores the conflation of guns and phalluses in the cultural imaginary when he writes, "guns and gun culture are phallocentric … They have always pivoted around men's power and men's pleasure. And although exceedingly homosocial, heterosexual difference and desire animate gun cultures as sexual cultures."[36] King's nexus of "men's pleasure," homosociality, and heterosexual difference, are played out in Limón's all-male staging of *The Emperor Jones*. One striking example occurs during Limón's first solo as Jones, when he is seated on his throne. Using his hands on the throne's armrests to support his weight, he remains seated, but twists and spirals his torso while gesturing with his legs and feet. During this movement sequence, he opens his legs wide and his pearl-handled pistol swings from the side of his hip to his crotch and becomes a dangling phallus. Limón removes his gun/phallus from his holster/crotch and embraces and strokes it. He brings it near to his mouth as if to whisper to it. This bold conflation of violence and sexuality reads in multiple ways. While the violence inherent in het-eronormative gun culture normalized *The Emperor Jones'* same-sex relations, it simultaneously served as a kind of deflective shield of signification that allowed Limón to dance his queer body, which granted subjectivity to non-normative characters and through them, himself.

Non-white universal bodies

In Chapter 4, I discussed Limón's performance in *Lament for Ignacio Sanchez Mejías* as a radical gesture breaking through conventions that had excluded non-white bodies from performing as a universal body. His performance of Sanchez Mejías as a universal Everyman compli-cated the perception that Euro-Americans possessed the exclusive privilege to embody universal themes. His performance in *The Emperor Jones* adds another layer of complexity. Unlike his prewar predecessors who used minstrel-based approaches to embody a general reference to a "pan-ethnic" culture, Limón's painted body in *The Emperor Jones* represented the singular and specific character of Brutus Jones. This specificity situates Jones as more than a timeless and "exotic" site on which to impose and express a transcendental universality. Limón's portrayal of Jones as an individual with the ability to experience shifting psychological states positioned him not only as a discursive site, or "site of the dramatic action," but also as the agent of the drama.[37]

Theatre scholar Julia Walker argues that *The Emperor Jones'* signifi-cance "lies not so much in the fact that its central character is black, as in the fact that, throughout the course of the play, he is shown to undergo a process of psychological change."[38] Walker's argument is as significant to prewar theatre as it is to postwar modern dance. Limón's portrayal of Jones as a character whose psychological make-up was not a fixed and essentialized part of his black body, allowed a specific non-white subject to transform in ways previously pro-hibited. In so doing, Limón's performance as Jones helps destabilize postwar biologically determinist views of African-Americans and offered a model for subsequent performers of color.

Although Limón's adaptation of *The Emperor Jones* took liberties with the play's casting and chronological structure, it follows O'Neill's text by placing the majority of the dance in the interior of the island jungle. And like O'Neill, Limón uses Jones' journey through the island interior as a way to stage Jones' shifting psychological interiority. In O'Neill's play, Jones discovers that his "native" subjects are planning to rebel, so he flees his palace, striking out on foot to the opposite side of the island where he has a boat waiting for just such an emergency. However, Jones loses his way and for the remainder of the play goes deeper into the dark recesses of the island jungle, and metaphorically, deeper into the dark recesses of his psychological interior.

Jones' struggle to find his way through the jungle to his boat, is exacerbated by his entanglement with what O'Neill calls "Little Formless Fears," hallucinatory entities that force him to relive troubled memories from his past. As Jones treks across the island, the Little Formless Fears torment and haunt him, causing him to lose his way. As a result of his response to the Little Formless Fears, Jones' personal history is gradually conflated with a broader pan-African collective history. For instance, in one scene, Jones is sold into slavery on an auction block and in another he is sacrificed at the altar of an African Crocodile God. Jones is finally shot by and killed by silver bullets especially prepared by his "rebel subjects." Limón's interventionist work of presenting a psychologically complex and transformative non-white individual is complicated by this essentialist move in O'Neill's text.

Conclusion

When Limón painted himself black, he painted himself into a corner. Adapting O'Neill's text was and remains a fraught venture. But perhaps the powerful contradictions and anxieties inherent in this adaptation were what drew Limón to the project. The volatile ways that race and gender move through O'Neill's text are fertile grounds for Limón's penchant to portray tragic, larger-than-life characters. This allure of O'Neill's play is akin to the allure of Alan Sinfield's notion of a "faultline story." Faultline stories are narratives of complex, contested issues that hinge upon unresolved ideological complications. Because they run so deep through social formations and are so integral to identity construction and community, faultline stories must be constantly re-invented and re-worked to serve changing frameworks. In similar ways to Hawkins' choreography in *Plains Daybreak*, Limón's re-working of prewar racial representational strategies was a final gasp for modern dance's naturalistic theatre. The issues of mobile, static, or hybrid cultural identities that Limón's tripled body brought to the fore, remain unresolved and continually challenged.

Notes

1 Danielson, Interview.
2 Manning 2004, 193.
3 Sparling, Interview.
4 Constance Valis Hill writes,

> Eddie Leonard (1883–1941) was considered one of the greatest minstrel men in vaudeville, having been a star of Haverly's Mastodon Minstrel troupe since the turn of the century. He was billed throughout his long career as the "Minstrel of the Hour."
>
> (Hill, *Tap Dancing America*, 62)

5 I use the term America and American anachronistically, to align it with the way that Limón used it to describe himself and the artform of American modern dance. Furthermore, I refer to Limón as Mexican or Mexican-American, but not as Latino, partly because he did not use that term and partly because it was not in wide circulation during his life. Neither do I refer to Limón as Chicano, again because he did not identify as such and also because he was not directly involved in Chicano activities.
6 Manning 2004, 193.
7 Although black paint was not used, brown and red hued paint was used by Denishawn in their dances based on "Oriental" and Native-American cultures.
8 Manning 2004, 10.
9 Tamiris did perform five sections of her *Negro Spirituals* for a one-time documentary filming in 1958.
10 Dixon-Gottschild, Citation, 84.
11 Dixon-Gottschild 1996, 84, italics in original.
12 Rogin 1996, 57, 58.
13 For a thorough discussion of O'Neill's relationship to whiteness, see Shannon Steen's "Melancholy Bodies: Racial Subjectivity and Whiteness in O'Neill's *The Emperor Jones*."
14 Lopez 2006, xxi.
15 Steen 2000, 343.
16 In a 1965 speech Limón entitled "The Universities and the Arts" he commented, "my present company of 22 dancers is composed almost

completely of my students, graduate and undergraduate, at Juilliard" Limón, *Dance Scope*, 26.

17 Stackhouse, Interview, Roth DVD.
18 Daniel Lewis, Interview.
19 O'Neill 1920, 9.
20 Monks 2005, 546, 547.
21 O'Neill 1920, 10.
22 Steen 2000, 356.
23 Jowitt 1972.
24 Hering quoted in Anderson 1987, 147.
25 Anderson 1987, 147.
26 Reviews of O'Neill's early production of *The Emperor Jones* can be found at, www.eoneill.com/index.htm.
27 The Wooster Group's production of *The Emperor Jones* in which actress Kate Valk performs the role of Brutus Jones in blackface provides a salient example.
28 Limón 1958, 38.
29 Kowal 2010, 40.
30 Burt 1995, 43.
31 See Foster's essay, "Closets Full of Dance: Modern Dance's Performance of Masculinity and Sexuality." In *Dancing Desires: Choreographing Sexualities On and Off the Stage*, Manning's chapter "Danced Spirituals." In *Modern Dance Negro Dance: Race in Motion*, and Foulkes's essay, "Dance Is for American Men: Ted Shawn and the Intersection of Gender, Sexuality and Nationalism in the 1930s." In *Dancing Desires: Choreographing Sexualities On and Off the Stage*.
32 Walter Terry, Lecture, 1975, MGZTC 3–2234.
33 Not included in this count are Limón's solo dances or his work in the US Army from 1943 to 1944. This puts Limón's first three all-male casts as *Diálogos* (1951), *The Traitor* (1954), and *Scherzo* (1955).
34 While duets were an integral part of Martha Graham's dances of the 1950s, they were primarily male/female duets.
35 Bogard 1988, 136.
36 King 2007, 88.
37 Walker 2009, 132.
38 Walker 2005, 132.

Works cited

Anderson, Jack. *The American Dance Festival*. Durham, NC: Duke University Press, 1987.

Bogard, Travis and Eugene O'Neill. *Contour in Time: The Plays of Eugene O'Neill*. New York: Oxford University Press, 1988.

Burt, Ramsay. *The Male Dancer: Bodies, Spectacle, Sexualities*. London: Routledge, 1995.

Certeau, Michel de, Luce Giard, and Pierre Mayol. *The Practice of Everyday Life*. Minneapolis, MN: University of Minnesota Press, 1998.

Dixon Gottschild, Brenda. *Digging the Africanist Presence in American Performance: Dance and Other Contexts.* Westport, CT: Greenwood Press, 1996.

Dyer, Richard. *White.* London: Routledge, 1997

Foster, Susan Leigh. "Closets Full of Dances: Modern Dance's Performance of Masculinity and Sexuality." In *Dancing Desires: Choreographing Sexualities on and Off the Stage,* edited by Jane Desmond. Madison, WI: University of Wisconsin Press, 2001.

Fox, Cybelle, and Thomas Guglielmo. "Defining America's Racial Boundaries: Blacks, Mexicans, and European Immigrants, 1890–1945." *American Journal of Sociology.* Vol. 118, No. 2. September 2012: 327–379.

Hill, Constance Valis. *Tap Dancing America.* New York: Oxford University Press, 2010.

Jowitt, Deborah. "Limón Pursues His Visions." *New York Times,* October 8, 1972.

King, Richard. "Arming Desire: The Sexual Force of Guns in the United States." In *Open Fire: Understanding Global Gun Cultures,* edited by Richard King. Oxford: Berg. 2007: 87–97.

Kowal, Rebekah. *How to do Things with Dance: Performing Change in Postwar America.* Middletown, CT: Wesleyan University Press, 2010.

Limón, José. "The Dancers' Status Here and Abroad: Comparisons and Observations." *Dance Observer.* March 1958: 37–39.

Limón, José. *A Life Beyond Words.* DVD. Dir. Malachi Roth. Frenchtown, NJ: Dance Conduit/Antidote Films, 2003.

Limón, José and Lynn Garafola. *José Limón: An Unfinished Memoir.* Hanover, NH: University Press of New England, 1998.

Lopez, Ian Haney. *White by Law: The Legal Construction of Race.* New York: NYU Press, 1997.

Manning, Susan. *Modern Dance, Negro Dance: Race in Motion.* Minneapolis, MN: University of Minnesota Press, 2004.

Monks, Aoife. "'Genuine Negroes and Real Bloodhounds:' Cross-Dressing, Eugene O'Neill, the Wooster Group, and The Emperor Jones." In *Modern Drama.* Vol. 48, No. 3. Fall 2005: 540–564.

O'Neill, Eugene. *The Emperor Jones. Anna Christie. The Hairy Ape.* New York: Vintage Books, 1972.

Pollock, Griselda. *Avant-Garde Gambits, 1888–1893: Gender and the Color of Art History.* New York: Thames and Hudson, 1993.

Rogin, Michael. *Blackface, White Noise: Jewish Immigrants in the Hollywood Melting Pot.* Berkeley, CA: University of California Press, 1998.

Sinfield, Alan. *Cultural Politics—Queer Reading.* Philadelphia, PA: University of Pennsylvania Press, 1994.

Stackhouse, Sarah. "The Director: Thoughts on Staging José Limón's La Malinche." In *José Limón and La Malinche: The Dancer and the Dance,* edited by Patricia Seed. Austin, TX: University of Texas Press. 2008: 154–165.

Steen, Shannon. "Melancholy Bodies: Racial Subjectivity and Whiteness in O'Neill's 'The Emperor Jones'." *Theatre Journal*. Vol. 52, No. 3. October 2000: 339–359.

Tsing, Anna. *Friction: An Ethnography of Global Connection.* Princeton, NJ: Princeton University Press, 2004.

Walker, Julia. *Expressionism and Modernism in the American Theatre: Bodies, Voices, Words.* New York: Cambridge University Press, 2009.

Index

Page numbers in *italics* denote figures.

T - #0037 - 050423 - C0 - 216/138/7 - PB - 9781032474588 - Gloss Lamination